Grace
from
Our Redeemer

Sermons for
Pentecost through Thanksgiving
Series B

David George Peters

DIET OF WORMS PRESS

Nelson, Wisconsin

Cover art courtesy of Avignon Art Studios of Racine, WI. Copyright © 2012 by the Rev. Dr. Nathan R. Pope, designer, and by Melanie Pope Schuette, artist. Used by permission.

All Scripture quotations, unless otherwise indicated, are from the Holy Bible, Evangelical Heritage Version ® (EHV ®) © 2019 Wartburg Project, Inc. All rights reserved. Used by permission. www.WartburgProject.org.

Scripture quotations marked "NIV" are taken from the Holy Bible, New International Version®. NIV®. Copyright © 1973, 1978, 1984, 2011 by Biblica, Inc.™ Used with permission of Zondervan. All rights reserved worldwide. www.Zondervan.com. The "NIV" and "New International Version" are trademarks registered in the United States Patent and Trademark Office by Biblica, Inc.™ www.Biblica.com.

All quotations of hymn lyrics and stanzas are taken from *Christian Worship: A Lutheran Hymnal.* © 1993 Northwestern Publishing House. www.NPH.net.

All catechetical quotations are taken from David P. Kuske, editor, *Luther's Catechism*, revised edition (Milwaukee: Northwestern Publishing House). Copyright © 1998 by the Board for Parish Services, Wisconsin Evangelical Lutheran Synod.

All rights reserved. No part of this publication may be copied, photocopied, reproduced, translated, or converted to any electronic or machine-readable form in whole or in part, except for brief quotations, without prior written approval from the publisher.

Diet of Worms Press

P.O. Box 23, Nelson, WI 54756

www.DietOfWormsPress.net

© 2024 David George Peters

First paperback edition, 2024

Printed in the USA

ISBN: 979-8-9894936-1-6

CONTENTS

Preface.. ix

THE PENTECOST SEASON

Pentecost Sunday...................................... 1
    Acts 2:12-13

The 1st Sunday after Pentecost: Trinity Sunday............ 7
    Matthew 28:16-20

The 2nd Sunday after Pentecost 14
    Colossians 2:13-17

The 3rd Sunday after Pentecost......................... 21
    Mark 3:20-35

The 4th Sunday after Pentecost......................... 28
    Mark 4:26-34

The 5th Sunday after Pentecost......................... 36
    Mark 4:35-41

The 6th Sunday after Pentecost......................... 41
    Lamentations 3:22-33

The 7th Sunday after Pentecost......................... 47
    2 Corinthians 12:7-10

The 8th Sunday after Pentecost......................... 53
    Amos 7:10-17

The 9th Sunday after Pentecost......................... 59
    Psalm 23

The 10th Sunday after Pentecost 64
    Mark 6:35-44

The 11th Sunday after Pentecost.................... 70
    John 6:24-35

The 12th Sunday after Pentecost 75
    1 Kings 19:3-8

The 13th Sunday after Pentecost 81
    Proverbs 9:1-6

The 14th Sunday after Pentecost 87
    John 6:60-69

The 15th Sunday after Pentecost 93
    Ephesians 6:10-20

The 16th Sunday after Pentecost 98
    Isaiah 35:4-7

The 17th Sunday after Pentecost 104
    James 2:14-26

The 18th Sunday after Pentecost 112
    Mark 9:30-37

The 19th Sunday after Pentecost 117
    Mark 9:38-50

The 20th Sunday after Pentecost..................... 124
    Mark 10:13-16

The 21st Sunday after Pentecost 130
    Mark 10:17-27

The 22nd Sunday after Pentecost..................... 137
    Hebrews 4:9-16

The 23rd Sunday after Pentecost..................... 142
    Mark 10:46-52

The 24th Sunday after Pentecost..................... 148
    Mark 12:28-34

The 25th Sunday after Pentecost..................... 153
    Hebrews 9:24-25

The 26th Sunday after Pentecost..................... 158
    Daniel 12:1-4

The 27th Sunday after Pentecost..................... 163
    Malachi 4:1-6

END OF THE YEAR FESTIVALS

The Last Sunday in September:
    The Festival of St. Michael and All Angels 169
        Matthew 18:1-11

The Last Sunday in October:
    Celebration of the Lutheran Reformation 176
        Jeremiah 18:1-11

The First Sunday in November:
    The Festival of All Saints......................... 182
        Isaiah 26:1-4,8-9,12-13,19-21

The Last Sunday of the Church Year:
    Christ the King Sunday........................... 189
        Daniel 7:13-14

A Festival of Thanksgiving 195
    Matthew 6:24-34

About the Author 201

PREFACE

Most people familiar with the life story of the sixteenth century church reformer Martin Luther are aware of his ten month stay in the Wartburg Castle near Eisenach, Saxony, where he was kept in protective custody immediately following the imperial "Diet of Worms." There Luther spent nearly all of his time meditating on God's Word, praying, and writing. His translation of the entire New Testament from Greek into German is his best known literary achievement at the Wartburg. However, for the first six months of his residency at the castle, Luther focused his writing on "postils" — books of sermons for the many priests and chaplains who were won for the evangelical cause and who left the Roman Catholic Church, but who had not been trained to be "Lutheran" preachers. Luther produced books of sermons for them to read to the people.

In addition to the works Luther penned at the Wartburg are several very important theological treatises as well as his voluminous correspondence with a few trusted individuals, especially his confidant Georg Spalatin, who was liaison to Luther's protector, the electoral Duke Frederick the Wise of Saxony.

This series of sermon books, however, will not deal with the writings of Martin Luther. Rather, this is a series of sermon books in the tradition of Luther's postils. But why write and publish these books of sermons?

I pray that these sermons will find a variety of good uses among God's people who love the grace that comes from our Redeemer, Jesus Christ. Many Christians will find spiritual edification by simply reading and pondering these sermons as a regular part of their weekly devotional practice. Those who are unable to attend regular worship services may choose to read these sermons for comfort and strength, especially men and women away from home in the military or at college, as well as homebound church members.

In our increasingly mobile society faithful Christian people sometimes find it necessary to move to parts of the country or even overseas where attendance at a faithful Christian church is not really feasible due to distance. Married couples, families, and even small Bible study groups may gather around the reading of these sermons for discussion and spiritual growth.

Pastors may use these sermons as commentaries on the texts for which they are preparing their own sermons. Seminary students and their professors may use some of these sermons as examples of what to do (and what not to do!) when composing their own sermons. God's people will certainly find other uses for these sermons which I cannot at this time even imagine.

Sadly, there is always a shortage of well-trained parish pastors available to serve Christian congregations. Our Redeemer pointed out this fact to his disciples and told them — and us! — to keep on praying for reapers (Matthew 9:38 and Luke 10:2). Some gatherings of Christians do not have a resident pastor and are accustomed to their worship being led by one or two laymen who are not trained in the art of sermon writing. This scenario is becoming increasingly common. On very rare occasions a pastor suffers an emergency or is otherwise absent from his pulpit when his congregation gathers for worship expecting to hear a Gospel-based sermon. In any event, these books of sermons can supply such a need for a lay leader to read an appropriate message from God's Word to God's people.

In 1521 Dr. Martin Luther, Augustinian, was called on the carpet before Emperor Charles V whose representatives demanded that Luther recant all that he had written. According to the historical tradition (which I prefer to believe is accurate), Luther responded:

I cannot and will not recant anything, for to go against conscience is neither right nor safe. Here I stand. I can do no other. God help me! Amen.[1]

The emperor was not pleased. On May 25, 1521, he banned all of Luther's writings and declared him to be a heretic and an enemy of the state. As an homage to the 500th anniversary of Luther's courageous confession at the city of Worms on the Upper Rhine, the Diet of Worms Press was founded on the Upper Mississippi in Nelson, Wisconsin, in the year of our Lord 2021. Plans are to publish

---

[1] Composite translation from a variety of English sources.

books of sermons, academic papers, and scholarly books — all in the spirit of classic Lutheran theology.

The title for this series of sermons has been carefully and thoughtfully selected. It has been my privilege to serve as a pastor and teacher in several Lutheran congregations and schools for the past thirty-six years, proclaiming our Redeemer's grace to Christians in Ohio, Nebraska, Kansas, Wisconsin, and Minnesota. Most recently I have thoroughly enjoyed the privilege of serving two small though beautiful congregations in the Upper Mississippi River Valley: Grace Evangelical Lutheran Church in Nelson, Wisconsin, and the Evangelical Lutheran Church of Our Redeemer in Wabasha, Minnesota. The names of these two congregations became the obvious name for this series of sermon books.

In 2020 I began to compile and edit these sermons during the quarantine which all but shut down our churches by order of the governors of Wisconsin and Minnesota (and most other American states) due to fear of the spread of SARS-CoV-2, the virus which causes "Covid-19." This began as a project to reach out with the Gospel to the members of my two congregations and then to others who might be willing to read or listen. I preached unedited versions of many of these sermons which were live streamed on Facebook. Some of them I printed, copied, and mailed out to church members, relatives, and friends, and to others on my church "prospect" mailing list. Yet it is my hope and expectation that all who read any or all of these sermons will grow in faith, knowledge, and understanding of our Redeemer's amazing grace.

It is not possible here to thank everyone who deserves recognition. My parents, Mr. and Mrs. James Terry and Elsie Peters, are responsible for introducing me to Jesus and leading me to the baptismal font at Grace Evangelical Lutheran Church in Tucson, Arizona. There I was catechized and confirmed by the Rev. E. Arnold Sitz and by several vicars who assisted him in ministry. My knowledge of our Redeemer's grace and his holy Word increased over the decades thanks to the excellent classical and theological education provided me at Martin Luther Academy (New Ulm, Minnesota), Northwestern College (Watertown, Wisconsin), Wisconsin Lutheran

Seminary (Mequon, Wisconsin), and Marquette University (Milwaukee, Wisconsin).

Several of my brothers in Gospel ministry reviewed portions or all of this manuscript and have provided me with excellent suggestions for improvement before publication. These fellow pastors include the Rev. Dr. Joel Pless of Wisconsin Lutheran College (Wauwatosa, Wisconsin) and the Rev. Dr. Nathan R. Pope of the First Evangelical Lutheran Church (Racine, Wisconsin). I cannot thank them enough for their evangelical insight and collegial input. Nevertheless, any and every shortcoming or error in this book is entirely my own.

I am especially grateful to my homiletics professors who taught me how to write and preach expository, thematic, evangelical Lutheran sermons. Those professors who very patiently taught me the theological languages of Latin and German as well as the biblical languages of Greek and Hebrew are responsible for my insight into and my exposition of the Holy Scriptures. My historical theology and church history professors taught me how to examine the past and to see the present in historical context, and they provided me with a framework for understanding how the eternal God in the fullness of time worked out the salvation of fallen mankind. My theological dogmatics professors taught me how to keep my doctrine straight, and my pastoral theology professors taught me what God's people really need to hear more than anything else in the whole world:

GRACE FROM OUR REDEEMER

John the Baptist, speaking about Our Redeemer:

"Out of his fullness we have all received grace upon grace. For the law was given through Moses; grace and truth came through Jesus Christ."

St. John 1:16-17

THE PENTECOST SEASON

Pentecost Sunday

TEXT: Acts 2:12-13

¹² They were all amazed and perplexed. They kept saying to one another, "What does this mean?" ¹³ But others mocked them and said, "They are full of new wine." ✠

The Word of the Lord. Thanks be to God!

In the name of Jesus, our crucified, risen, and ascended Redeemer, my dear Christian friends:

At the Tower of Babel, God scrambled the languages of mankind — a powerful miracle, indeed. On Pentecost Sunday, several thousand years later, God temporarily reversed what he had done at Babel. Rather than scrambling human languages, God gave certain men the miraculous ability to preach the wonderful works of God in foreign languages which they had never studied. Those disciples of Jesus went out into the streets of Jerusalem and proclaimed God's Word to God's people, most of whom came from far away lands:

- ☞ Parthians = from Afghanistan
- ☞ Medes = from northern Iran
- ☞ Elamites = from southern Iran
- ☞ Mesopotamians = from Iraq and perhaps Kuwait
- ☞ A bunch of people from the land we call Turkey: from Cappadocia, Pontus, Asia, Phrygia, and Pamphilia
- ☞ Judeans = those were the local Jews
- ☞ A bunch of people from North Africa: Egyptians and Libyans
- ☞ People from the city of Rome
- ☞ People from the island of Crete

☞ Not just people with Jewish blood in their veins, but also many converts to Judaism

☞ And yes, there were even some Arabs in the crowd!

Those people were almost all tourists on a spiritual pilgrimage to Israel in order to celebrate "Pentecost," the offering of the first fruits of their spring harvest at the temple of the LORD in Jerusalem. Remember, about 90% of the Jews lived outside of the Holy Land; so this was, for most of them, a once in a lifetime trip to Jerusalem.

And what did they see there? Those Jewish pilgrims saw about one hundred and twenty of Jesus' followers standing in the streets, preaching the wonderful works of the LORD in the native languages of the pilgrims — foreign tongues which they had never studied. Wow! This was not just some ecstatic babbling of nonsense syllables! These were real languages — the languages of those thousands of visitors.

If I were to begin preaching to you in Spanish or German, that would not be an example of speaking in tongues for two reasons: Those are not your native tongue, and I have studied those languages for many years. But if you were a Japanese person and all of a sudden I began preaching God's Word to you in your native language, that would be a miracle of God because I have never studied Japanese.

And that was the first miracle of Pentecost. The Holy Spirit descended upon Jesus' Church and temporarily reversed the curse of Babel. He jump-started the spread of the Gospel to the whole world by enabling his disciples to proclaim the message of Jesus in many foreign languages they had never studied — in the native tongues of all those Pentecost pilgrims. In words so often used by Martin Luther:

What Does This Mean?

What happened in Jerusalem on that particular Pentecost was a great miracle! Several thousand witnesses could testify to that. But what does that Pentecost miracle mean for you and me? We are going to explore that today.

The Pentecost Season

Before Pentecost Jesus had about one hundred and twenty disciples — people who followed and supported him because they believed him to be God's long-promised Messiah. On Pentecost Sunday the Holy Spirit miraculously converted to faith in Jesus about three thousand more people who heard the Gospel preached in their own languages in the streets of Jerusalem. Those new converts were immediately baptized. This was the second miracle of Pentecost! The number of Jesus' disciples continued to grow every day thereafter as they shared their new-found faith with the non-Christian people around them. The Spirit used that Gospel message which Jesus' disciples proclaimed to create faith in the hearts of many, many more people.

That is still how the Holy Spirit works! That's how God saves people from eternal damnation. That's how God converts unbelievers into believers and saves their souls for eternity. In short, that's the only way that anybody can get to heaven — by God's people spreading the good news of Jesus, and by baptizing the nations — by the Holy Spirit using their Gospel testimony and the Sacrament of Baptism to call people to trust in Jesus for salvation.

The Holy Spirit saved you and me in the very same way. Luther explains this in his *Small Catechism* in his definition of the Third Article of the Apostles' Creed:

> I believe that I cannot by my own thinking or choosing
> > believe in Jesus Christ, my Lord, or come to him.
> But the Holy Spirit has called me by the Gospel,
> > enlightened me with his gifts,
> > sanctified and kept me in the true faith.
> In the same way he calls, gathers, enlightens and sanctifies
> > the whole Christian Church on earth,
> > and keeps it with Jesus Christ in the one true faith.

Yes, the Holy Spirit has also called <u>you</u> by the Gospel, enlightened <u>you</u> with his gifts, sanctified and kept <u>you</u> in the one true faith — faith in Jesus as the Savior — faith in the Son of the living God, who suffered and died to atone for every one of your sins — faith in Christ Jesus, who rose back to life from the grave to declare you forgiven and to assure you of eternal life in heaven. Yes,

Part 1: The Holy Spirit Called <u>You</u> to be a Disciple of Jesus!

But what <u>is</u> a "disciple," anyway? A disciple is a student, a follower, and a learner. A disciple follows his master teacher and listens to him teach and preach. He observes his teacher's lifestyle. He adopts his teacher's outlook on life, his attitudes, and even his very words. A disciple strives to copy his teacher's way of life, to put into practice his master's teachings. Once he has the hang of it, a disciple turns around and tells others what he has learned from his master, the teachings which he has become convinced are the truth. That's what a disciple is.

The Holy Spirit also called <u>you</u> to be a disciple of Jesus! He did that through the very same Means of Grace by which he called three thousand new disciples on Pentecost. He led you to be baptized in the name of the Father, Son, and Holy Spirit, and he has continued to teach you the Gospel of Jesus ever since your baptism. Right now you are experiencing some continuing education as a faithful disciple of your master Teacher, your Redeemer, Jesus Christ. And,

Part 2: The Holy Spirit Has Taught You the Basic Truths of the Faith!

Jesus taught his twelve disciples for over three years with 'round-the-clock intensive instruction, yet they still had much to learn. Just ten days before Pentecost, on the mount of his ascension, they asked Jesus that bone-head question: *"Lord, is this the time when you are going to restore the kingdom to Israel?"*[1] They still didn't get it. They needed continuing education. They needed the Holy Spirit to teach them what they still needed to know and believe.

So Jesus responded to their silly question:

<u>Acts 1:7-8</u>: *[7]"It is not for you to know the times or seasons that the Father has set by his own authority. [8] But you will receive power when the Holy Spirit has come upon you, and you will be my witnesses in Jerusalem, in all Judea and Samaria, and to the ends of the earth."*

---

[1] Acts 1:6

Jesus promised his disciples that he would send them the Holy Spirit, and that the Spirit would enable them to serve as his witnesses throughout the world.

Every one of you has been taught the basics of the Christian faith. At your confirmation you publicly confessed your faith in those basic truths. Yet those are just the basics! As we grow into adulthood we need to move on from the milk to the meat — not giving up the milk, but learning more and more about the teachings of our Lord Jesus as they are spelled out for us in the Holy Scriptures.

As long as you live, you will never know the whole counsel of God. The Bible is far too big a book for anyone to know everything, so we all have plenty more to learn. So then, how do you put Jesus' teachings into practice in your life as one of his disciples?

Part 3: The Holy Spirit Enables You to Live as a Disciple of Jesus!

Okay. So now I'm a disciple of Jesus. I am a child of God. How should I then live? What does God expect of me? What does he demand of me? Perfection? Yes, God demands perfection — but nobody's perfect, right? And holiness? Yes, God demands that we live holy lives — but I am far from holy. So is everybody I know. I look at God's Ten Commandments and I see that there's <u>no way</u> that I can be perfectly holy. Woe is me! What can I do about my failures, my weakness, my shortcomings — my sins?

Calm down! Don't despair! You see, this is the beauty of Christianity. God already knows all that stuff. He knows our weaknesses, our failures, our shortcomings, our sins — and yet he loves us nevertheless. So our Heavenly Father sent his Son Jesus into this world to live that perfect life <u>for us</u>, in our place. Jesus lived a holy life <u>for us</u>. Through faith in him and in his saving work, God credits Jesus' perfection, his holiness, <u>to us</u>! Jesus suffered and died to pay the penalty which you and I rightly deserved because of our countless sins, and Jesus has atoned for them all. He went to the cross voluntarily, where he laid down his life for us and for the whole human race. Two days later he rose back to life and declared his victory over sin, over death, and over the power of the devil. All of this Jesus did for you and for me and for all people of all time.

So be of good cheer! Our gracious Lord has put away your sins. Every single one of them has been forgiven. That same Jesus who took the burden of your guilt upon himself and paid for every sin, now consoles your spirit with his loving compassion and tender mercy, and he blesses you with the gift of his Spirit.

And this Holy Spirit, who proceeds from the Father and the Son, enables us to live as disciples of Jesus and as co-heirs of eternal life with him in heaven. The Spirit has called us into his Holy Christian Church for time and for eternity. Our *Catechism* lays it out for us in simple terms:

> In this Christian Church he daily and fully forgives all sins
> to me and all believers.
> On the Last Day he will raise me and all the dead; and he
> will give eternal life to me and all believers in Christ.
> This is most certainly true.

Thank you, Jesus, O gracious Redeemer, for giving us your Holy Spirit! Help us to live as disciples who are worthy of your holy name, and keep us steadfast in the one true faith! AMEN.

The 1ˢᵗ Sunday after Pentecost: Trinity Sunday

TEXT: Matthew 28:16-20

¹⁶ The eleven disciples went to Galilee, to the mountain where Jesus had directed them. ¹⁷ When they saw him, they worshipped him, but some hesitated because they were uncertain. ¹⁸ Jesus approached and spoke to them saying, "All authority in heaven and on earth has been given to me. ¹⁹ Therefore, go and gather disciples from all nations by baptizing them in the name of the Father and of the Son and of the Holy Spirit, ²⁰ and by teaching them to keep all the instructions I have given you. And surely I am with you always until the end of the age." ✠

The Gospel of our Lord. Praise be to you, O Christ!

In the name of the Triune God, my dear fellow Christians:

Countless people over the centuries have tried either to discover God or to invent a god of their own:

- Some, like the American Indians, believed that their gods are to be found in every rock, in every mountain and river, and even in the wind.

- Others, like the ancient Greeks and Romans, thought that a bunch of gods lived up on top of Mount Olympus, and that they occasionally came down to interact with humans — sometimes even having children by human women. The resulting children were half god and half man, such as Hercules, the son of Zeus and Princess Alcmene. (Of course, this is all just ancient Greek and Roman mythology, but countless millions of people believed that stuff! That mythology was their religion.)

- As many people grew to reject that stuff, they turned to human wisdom and philosophy. Some philosophers, such as Plato and his followers, taught that "god" is the great, transcendent "Mind" who emanated a thought, and that <u>thought</u> (they called it the "*Logos*") created a slightly imperfect world which has been running downhill ever since. You see, the Mind did not do the creating; the *Logos* did — and the *Logos* is beneath the Mind and is not quite as perfect as the Mind. The Mind was Plato's perfect god. (But you didn't come here to learn philosophy, did you?)

☞ Some, like the Hindus, believe that there are many — even millions — of gods (Krishna and Vishnu being the most famous).

☞ Countless billions have bowed down to their own gods of wood and stone which were fashioned by human hands.

☞ Some, like the Mormons, believe that there are many gods, and that every god used to be a man. They teach that the god of planet earth, whom they call "our Heavenly Father," was once a man who lived such an upright and holy life that, when he died, he was promoted to become a god himself and was given his own planet to populate and govern. This is how all gods came to be (so they say). The Mormons believe that <u>all</u> worthy Mormon men will themselves become gods of their own planets some day, and that they and their wives will spend eternity populating their own planet.

☞ Jews and Muslims believe correctly that there is only one true God (they're right about that, so far); but both of those groups worship a <u>unitarian</u> god, not the Trinitarian God — so they each worship an idol of their own making.

With so many different concepts of God, how can we possibly know <u>who</u> the one true God <u>is</u>? Who is that one true God, the maker of all people and of everything that exists? Who is the one true God in whom we should believe and whom we must worship?

Well, I have good news for you! The one true God has revealed himself in the Holy Bible, and he has revealed himself in the person of Jesus of Nazareth. The Bible reveals to us and to the whole world:

The Mystery of the Holy Trinity

Shortly before his ascension back into heaven, the risen Christ met with his disciples on a mountain in the Galilee. There, in verse 19 of our text, he commissioned his New Testament Church to *"gather disciples from all nations by baptizing them in the name of the Father, and of the Son, and of the Holy Spirit...."*

This is how Jesus identifies the one true God. This is how Jesus defines God for us. We are not to baptize people into the name of some other god, but into the name of the Triune God: the Father, the Son, and the Holy Spirit. And this is the God into whose name every Christian has been baptized ever since. So:

Part 1: Worshipping Any "God," Other than the One True God, Is Worshipping a False God.

In other words, it's idolatry. Sadly, most human beings invent their own gods rather than believing in the one true God who revealed himself to his own world in his Holy Scriptures. What do you suppose the Creator and Savior thinks about that? He tells us in Isaiah 42: *"I am the LORD; that is my name. I will not give my glory to another, nor my praise to idols."* [1] God is very protective of his glory and of his holy name. He protects his glory in his First Commandment, when he says: *"You shall have no other gods beside me!"* [2] And the LORD protects his holy name with his Second Commandment: *"You shall not misuse the name of the LORD your God!"* [3]

So then, according to his own testimony, there is only one true God, and:

Part 2: That One and Only True God Is the Holy Trinity!

---

[1] Isaiah 42:8
[2] Exodus 20:3
[3] Exodus 20:7

Now it's true that there is a certain unity, a certain oneness, about the one true God. He says in Deuteronomy chapter 6: *"Hear, O Israel! The LORD is our God. The LORD is one!"*[4] The prophet Malachi writes: *"Don't we all have one Father? Hasn't one God created us?"*[5] The implied answers to his rhetorical questions are obviously: Why yes, of course! We do all have the same Father, and one God did create us all!

St. Paul writes to the Romans: *"There is only one God."*[6] Paul writes to the Ephesians: *"There is one Lord, one faith, one baptism, one God and Father of all, who is over all, and through all, and in us all."*[7] And to the Corinthians Paul writes: *"There is but one God, the Father, from whom all things came and for whom we live."*[8]

St. James says it this way: *"You believe that there is one God. Good! Even the demons believe that — and shudder."*[9]

So, both the Old Testament and the New Testament clearly teach MONOTHEISM: that there is only one true God, and he is the creator of all people and of all things. POLYTHEISM, the notion that multiple gods exist, is clearly denied through the entire Bible.

Yet there is also a certain PLURALITY about the one true God. In the opening chapters of Genesis Moses tells us about the beginning of all things. After creating everything else, it was time for God to create human beings. *"God said, 'Let us make man in our image, according to our likeness."*[10] Do you hear those plural words "us" and "our"? There must also be something plural about God!

On Mt. Sinai God commanded the high priests of Israel to bless all of his people by raising their hands over them and speaking these words: *"The LORD bless you and keep you; the LORD make his face shine on you and be gracious to you; the LORD look on you with*

---

[4] Deuteronomy 6:4
[5] Malachi 2:10
[6] Romans 3:30 (NIV)
[7] Ephesians 4:5-6
[8] 1 Corinthians 8:6
[9] James 2:19
[10] Genesis 1:26

The Pentecost Season

favor and give you peace."[11] (Christian pastors very often use those same words to bless God's people today.)

All three persons of the Holy Trinity revealed themselves at Jesus' baptism. There was Jesus, the Second Person of the Trinity, standing in the river. The Third Person, the Holy Spirit, descended upon Jesus in the form of a dove, while the First Person, the Heavenly Father, boomed his voice down from the heavens, saying: *"This is my Son, whom I love. I am well pleased with him."*[12]

After his resurrection but before his ascension, Jesus spoke the words of our text in his Great Commission, commanding his Church to baptize the nations *"... in the name of the Father, and of the Son, and of the Holy Spirit."* Notice that Jesus spelled out all three persons of the Holy Trinity as equally <u>God</u> into whose name we are to baptize and to be baptized.

St. Paul concluded his second letter to the Corinthians with this benediction: *"The grace of the Lord Jesus Christ, and the love of God, and the fellowship of the Holy Spirit be with you all."*[13] In these words Paul spells out the three persons of the Holy Trinity.

So <u>who</u> exactly <u>is</u> God? Idol worshipers don't know — neither do philosophers, nor do evolutionists. Nobody can dream up the almighty God, nor conjure him up in our puny human brains. If you or I would set out to design or invent our own religion, there's no way that we would invent such a God! The very nature of God — three unique persons in one divine Being — is far beyond human comprehension. The one true God is Father, Son, and Holy Spirit. God is THREE, and yet God is ONE. Got it? I don't! The essence of the Creator and Sustainer of this entire universe is far too vast for any mortal to grasp.

Christianity speaks of three self-subsisting Persons in one Divine Being: <u>not</u> three gods, <u>nor</u> God by committee; <u>not</u> one god who reveals himself in three different ways at various times and places, <u>nor</u> three unique persons who are each one-third of God. These are all heresies which the Christian Church has consistently rejected and

---

[11] Numbers 6:24-26
[12] Matthew 3:17
[13] 2 Corinthians 13:14

condemned at nearly every council of the Church since Nicæa in A.D. 325. They are <u>heresies</u> because, even though they may <u>seem</u> to explain the nature and essence of God in ways that people can understand, they all violate multiple passages of the Holy Scriptures and make God out to be less than one, true, eternal, indivisible, almighty Being. <u>But</u>:

- ☞ the one true God, who created and preserves us to this very day; and
- ☞ the one true God who saved us from sin and eternal damnation; and
- ☞ the one true God who called us by the Gospel, enlightened us with his gifts, sanctified us, and kept us in the one true faith,

<u>is</u> the Holy Trinity: the Father, the Son, and the Holy Spirit. This is most certainly true!

And this is most certainly a <u>mystery</u>. No human mind dreamed this up. This is what God teaches us about himself through his chosen prophets, apostles, and evangelists. This is how God has revealed himself in his sacred Word, the Holy Bible.

All other so-called "gods" are idols — false gods, that is. And no god but the Triune God <u>saves</u> anybody for time and for eternity! In the words of St. Peter: *"There is salvation in no one else, for there is no other name under heaven given to people by which we must be saved."*[14] The Triune God not only <u>created</u> us, but he also <u>saves</u> us through the blood of Jesus Christ, which cleanses us from all our sins. The Second Person of the Holy Trinity lived for us, died for us, and rose back to life for us in order to buy us back from sin, from death, and from the power of the Devil. The Third Person of the Holy Trinity called us by the Gospel, enlightened us with his gifts, sanctified us, and keeps us in the one true faith.

Praise be to the Triune God for making us, for rescuing us from eternal damnation, for calling us to be his children, for washing away our sins in Holy Baptism, and for strengthening us in our Christian

---

[14] Acts 4:12

faith, so that we can spend eternity with Jesus in the heavenly mansions which he is preparing for us right now. AMEN.

The 2ⁿᵈ Sunday after Pentecost

TEXT: Colossians 2:13-17

¹³ Even when you were dead in your trespasses and the uncircumcision of your flesh, God made you alive with Christ by forgiving us all our trespasses. ¹⁴ God erased the record of our debt brought against us by his legal demands. This record stood against us, but he took it away by nailing it to the cross. ¹⁵ After disarming the rulers and authorities, he made a public display of them by triumphing over them in Christ.

¹⁶ Therefore, do not let anyone judge you in regard to food or drink, or in regard to a festival or a New Moon or a Sabbath day. ¹⁷ These are a shadow of the things that were coming, but the body belongs to Christ. ✠

The Word of the Lord. Thanks be to God!

In the name of Jesus, dear Christian friends:

I was once told by a Seventh Day Adventist: "You Christians had no right changing the Sabbath Day! God commanded that Saturday must be the Sabbath Day, but you Christians changed it to Sunday. You violate the Bible!"

What do <u>you</u> think? Was he right? Or was he wrong? Does it matter? Let's see what the Bible has to say about the Sabbath Day for us New Testament Christians. Did the early Christian Church change the Sabbath Day? What exactly IS the Sabbath Day? And why does any of this matter to us?

Let's face it: God did indeed establish one day each week as a day of rest — the Sabbath Day. So, since God established it, it is certainly fair to say that:

We Have No Business Changing the Sabbath Day!

I think that we should all be able to agree on that. After all, when we look back at the Old Testament Law of Moses, this is perfectly clear:

Part 1: God Certainly <u>Did</u> Establish Saturday as the Sabbath for His <u>Old</u> Testament People.

When God engraved his Third Commandment onto stone tablets with his own finger, he also gave his reasons for establishing a weekly Day of Rest. As Moses wrote in:

<u>Exodus 20:8-11</u>: *Remember the Sabbath day by setting it apart as holy. Six days you are to serve and do all your regular work, but the seventh day shall be a Sabbath rest to the LORD your God. Do not do any regular work, neither you, nor your sons or daughters, nor your male or female servants, nor your cattle, nor the alien who is residing inside your gates, for in six days the LORD made the heavens and the earth, the sea, and everything that is in them, but he rested on the seventh day. In this way the LORD blessed the seventh day and made it holy.*

So God himself worked during the six days of creation, but then he stopped and did not work on the seventh day. Then God used his own example as the model for our work week. We may work for six days, but then we must rest regularly and faithfully, just as God did. This provides rest for our souls as well as our bodies. This is what made the seventh day "holy." It was a day set aside by God for God's use and for God's purposes!

Now what does that word "holy" mean? We usually think of it as meaning "sinless" — but it means much more than that. It means "set apart for God and for his use only."

This Sabbath command was part of the ceremonial law code which God gave to Old Testament Israel. That ceremonial part of the Law of Moses governed the religious ceremonies which linked God and his chosen people together. It was full of object lessons and images of the coming Messiah who would rescue them from sin and eternal damnation. Those ceremonial laws kept the people of Israel close to the one true God, the Creator and Savior. Those laws also kept God's people separate from the heathen nations around them who did not worship the one true God. In short, the ceremonial law was a great blessing for the Old Testament Jews.

Part 2: But We Are <u>Not</u> Old Testament Jews!

We are New Testament Christians, so the laws which governed the religious ceremonies of Old Testament Israel don't apply to us! How do we know that? St. Paul says in:

<u>Verses 16-17</u>: *¹⁶Do not let anyone judge you in regard to food or drink, or in regard to a festival or a New Moon or a Sabbath day. ¹⁷These are a <u>shadow</u> of the things that were coming, but the body belongs to Christ.*

So the Old Testament Sabbath, as with all the other Old Testament signs and symbols, <u>foreshadowed</u> Jesus Christ, the Messiah who would someday come into the world to fulfill them — to save God's people from their sins — to save <u>us</u> from <u>our</u> sins!

And Jesus finally DID come and fulfill all of those shadows for us, didn't he? Now that he has already come and done his saving work, we have the <u>reality</u> — we have Jesus himself — and we no longer need shadows to teach us about a Savior to come. He has already been here! Paul also says that *"The law was our chaperone <u>until Christ</u>, so that we might be justified by faith. But now that this faith has come, we are no longer under a chaperone."*[1]

Since the purpose of the Old Testament Sabbath has been fulfilled, we ought never let anybody judge and condemn us for no longer observing Saturday as God's prescribed Day of Rest. Christ Jesus has freed us from the Law of Moses, including the requirements of the Ceremonial Law. We are not saved by obeying God's Ceremonial Law. We are not saved by obeying any of the Law of Moses or by obeying any Law at all! Law can only kill and condemn. It can't save anybody, for we are all law breakers. We are all sinners.

But here is Good News which Paul spells out so graphically in:

<u>Verses 13-15</u>: *¹³Even when you were dead in your trespasses and the uncircumcision of your flesh, God made you alive with Christ by forgiving us all our trespasses. ¹⁴God erased*

---

[1] Galatians 3:24-25

the record of our debt brought against us by his legal demands. This record stood against us, but he took it away by nailing it to the cross. ^{15}After disarming the rulers and authorities, he made a public display of them by triumphing over them in Christ.

God took that rap sheet which listed all of our sins — every violation of his legal demands — and God nailed that rap sheet to the cross with Christ. It has been paid for, as St. John says: *"The blood of Jesus Christ, God's Son, cleanses us from all sins."*[2]

But you and I are not Old Testament Jews, so that Ceremonial Law code no longer applies to us. We are New Testament Christians, and we have been freed from the Law by Christ! Yet the Ten Commandments still <u>do</u> apply to us New Testament Christians today, and that includes the 3rd Commandment. How so?

Well, the Ten Commandments are ten specific applications of God's holy Law of Love, and that is not Ceremonial Law. It is God's Moral Law, which never expires. The Moral Law is for all people of all time. It is still God's will that all of his people enjoy Sabbath rest. Yet in the New Testament God gives us the freedom to pick the days and times ourselves. The Book of Hebrews says:

<u>Hebrews 4:9-11</u>: *There remains a Sabbath rest for the people of God. For the one who enters God's rest also rests from his own work, just as God rested from his work. Therefore, let us make every effort to enter that rest, so that no one will fall into the same pattern of disobedience.*

Did you ever notice that the Third Commandment is the <u>only</u> Commandment about which God felt the need to remind us: "Now <u>don't forget</u> this one!" "*<u>Remember</u> to keep the Sabbath Day holy!*" REMEMBER THIS! AND DON'T FORGET IT!

Martin Luther understood this matter perfectly. He beautifully defines the Third Commandment for us in his *Small Catechism*:

Remember to keep the Sabbath Day holy!

What does this mean?

---

[2] 1 John 1:7

> We should fear and love God that we do not despise preaching and his Word, but regard it as holy, and gladly hear and learn it.

The preaching of God's Word is what is holy and sacred. Missing a worship service once in a while because you are sick, or because there's a terrible epidemic, or because you must do works of mercy by caring for the sick or infirm, or because you must be out of town on a given weekend — none of that is sinful in and of itself; but despising the preaching of God's holy Word <u>is</u> sin! God doesn't care about what day we meditate on his holy Word. <u>Any</u> day you do that <u>is</u> holy because God's Word is holy. Failing to give God's Word and Sacraments top priority in your life is sin. Yet forgiveness of sins and eternal salvation are found only in the Gospel of Jesus Christ.

Jesus told the Jews that faithful children of God listen to God's Word, and that those who do not listen to his Word — those who do not consider God's Word to be holy — are not faithful Christians! Jesus says: *"Whoever belongs to God listens to what God says. The reason you do not listen is that you do not belong to God."*[3]

Let's be honest. None of us has always loved God and his Word most of all. Often we consider it a drudgery to get up, get dressed, and go to church or Sunday School, or to read our Bible or *Meditations*, or listen to the pastor whom God has sent us to teach and preach the Word of God. We often find other things to do which seem more pressing, more fun, or more lucrative. The Devil tempts us with all sorts of activities which are not in and of themselves sinful, but they <u>become</u> sins for us if they tear us away from hearing God's Word on a regular basis: ball games, fishing, hunting, vacations, golf — and I love all those activities, too! But if Satan uses them as stumbling blocks between us and the only means by which God gives us his grace (the Gospel in Word and Sacraments), then those activities become sinful for us.

Don't forget to keep the Sabbath day holy — that means regularly setting aside time for God and his Word! As the Good Book says: *"Let us not neglect meeting together, as some have the habit*

---

[3] John 8:47

of doing. Rather, let us encourage each other, and all the more as you see the Day approaching."[4]

Let's face it. Not one of us is perfectly holy, neither in this respect nor in any other. St. Paul says that: *"All have sinned and fall short of the glory of God."*[5] That's God's Law! But in the very next verse Paul proclaims God's Gospel: *"... and all are justified freely by his grace through the redemption that is in Christ Jesus."*[6]

Jesus invites us — and he invites every sinner:

Matthew 11:28-30: *[28] Come to me, all you who are weary and burdened, and I will give you Shabbat — Sabbath — rest. [29] Take my yoke upon you and learn from me, for I am gentle and humble in heart, and you will find rest for your souls. [30] For my yoke is easy and my burden is light.*

Jesus is saying to us: "Do you want true Sabbath rest? I am the One who gives you true Sabbath rest! Come to me! I am your Sabbath! You will only find true rest in me!"

Now that summer is here, don't forget to keep the Sabbath day holy. Set apart regular time to listen to God's holy Word and to receive God's holy Sacrament. When you are away from home and unable to attend our church services on Sundays, look up the nearest congregation of our fellowship and worship with them! Take your Bible, your prayer book, your *Meditations* booklet, your catechism, your hymnal, and spend some time every day reading and meditating on the Gospel of our Savior Jesus. In his Words you will find food for your soul, forgiveness of your sins, direction for daily living, strength to face your daily challenges, comfort in times of sorrow, and inspiration leading to eternal life.

For Old Testament Jews the Sabbath Day was every Saturday and every religious festival as prescribed in the Law of Moses. But for us New Testament Christians, the Sabbath Day is every time we spend time with God's holy Word and Sacraments. Don't forget to

---

[4] Hebrews 10:25
[5] Romans 3:23
[6] Romans 3:24

keep the Sabbath Day holy! For you will always find true rest in the Gospel Jesus Christ. AMEN.

THE PENTECOST SEASON

The 3ʳᵈ Sunday after Pentecost

TEXT: Mark 3:20-35

[20] They went into a house. A crowd gathered again so that they were not even able to eat a meal. [21] When his own people heard this, they went out to take control of him, because they were saying, "He is out of his mind."

[22] The experts in the law who came down from Jerusalem were saying, "He is possessed by Beelzebul," and "He drives out demons by the ruler of demons."

[23] Jesus called them together and spoke to them in parables. "How can Satan drive out Satan? [24] If a kingdom is divided against itself, that kingdom cannot stand. [25] And if a house is divided against itself, that house cannot stand. [26] And if Satan has risen up against himself and is divided, he cannot stand but is finished. [27] On the other hand, no one can enter a strong man's house to steal his possessions unless he ties up the strong man first. Then he can plunder his house. [28] Amen I tell you: Everything will be forgiven people, their sins and whatever blasphemies they may speak. [29] But whoever blasphemes against the Holy Spirit will never have forgiveness, but is guilty of an eternal sin." [30] Jesus said this because they were saying, "He has an unclean spirit."

[31] Then his mother and his brothers arrived. While they were standing outside, they sent word to Jesus, calling for him. [32] A crowd was sitting around him. They began to tell him, "Look, your mother and your brothers are outside looking for you."

[33] He replied, "Who are my mother and my brothers?" [34] He looked at those who sat around him in a circle and he said, "Look, my mother and my brothers! [35] For whoever does the will of God is my brother and sister and mother." ✠

The Gospel of our Lord. Praise be to you, O Christ!

In the name of our Brother Jesus, my dear brothers and sisters:

Several of our nation's founding fathers were not Christians, but "deists" — most notably Thomas Jefferson and Benjamin Franklin.

The basic idea of "deism" is that "god," as they understand him, began his work of creation as a boy spins a top; then he just stood back to watch, and even now watches us from a distance to see what happens. Deism is the idea that "god" is a very long way off — far too transcendent to be imminent. In other words, God is too far away to be intimately concerned about our lives or to have much influence in our world.

Deists are quite comfortable staying away from God's holy Word and Sacraments because they see no need for them and are not terribly interested in them. After all, they figure, their version of "god" is not terribly interested in us. They believe that the Bible is only of value as a bunch of neat fables and quotable quotes, and for several ethical principles which the reader may find on its pages.

Deists believe that we human beings have the ability to span the vast gulf between ourselves and "god," to find "god" and to commune with him any time we want to, but on <u>our own</u> terms. Yet deists deny "god" that same ability to span the great distance between himself and his creatures, and they deny "god" the ability to deal with us on <u>his</u> terms.

Deists deny that any "god" created mankind in his own image. They insist that we must envision "god" on <u>our own</u> terms — that each of us creates "god" in whatever image <u>we</u> choose. In short, deists have little use for any claims that the Bible is true, or that it is even the Word of God.

In our sermon text today we hear about three different families. Two of those families were like a bunch of deists who had little use for the Words of Jesus because they did not believe Jesus to be the Son of God. But this text also tells us about a third family. The question I want you to answer for yourself this morning is this:

To Which Family Do YOU Belong?

Family #1? Family #2? or Family #3?

Family #1:

The first family we'll consider today is Jesus' own biological family. The Bible records their names for us: Jesus' mother Mary, his four half-brothers, and his two half-sisters.[1] Today's Gospel Lesson tells us about a time when his biological family thought that they would bail Jesus out of the tough jam in which he found himself, surrounded by people who had cornered him in a house, many of whom did not like him and who accused him of blasphemy. The Law of Moses prescribed death by stoning for all blasphemers.

At this time Jesus' biological family does not yet understand him. In fact, they seem embarrassed by his notoriety. They try to excuse him by explaining away what he has been preaching and doing, telling their fellow Jews: *"Don't pay any attention to him! He is out of his mind! He's crazy!"* They try to extract Jesus from a hot situation. They are not at all interested in his teaching and preaching. That's Family #1.

Family #2:

Family #2 you might say is Jesus' own "church family." They are represented in our Gospel lesson by the *"experts in the Law"* of Moses. They are those pesky theologians whom the King James Version usually calls the *"scribes."* They accuse Jesus of using Satan's own power to exorcize demons. They accuse Jesus of being demon possessed himself, saying: *"He is possessed by Beelzebul."* They try to discredit Jesus in the minds of his hearers in order to shrink the number of people who follow him.

So Jesus demonstrates the illogic of their argument. He says in:

Verses 23-26:   *²³ "How can Satan drive out Satan? ²⁴ If a kingdom is divided against itself, that kingdom cannot*

---

[1] Four biological brothers of Jesus are mentioned by name in the New Testament, which also says that they had sisters (Matthew 13:55-56). They were all the natural children of Joseph and Mary, born after Jesus' virginal conception and birth. James became an early leader of the Christian church at Jerusalem (cf. Acts 12:17; 15:13-29; 21:18; *et al.*) and wrote the Epistle of St. James. The Holy Spirit inspired Judas to write the Epistle of St. Jude. Joseph (Matthew 13:55) is also called Joses (Mark 6:3). Simon is only mentioned by name in Matthew 13:55. The Bible does not give the names of any of their sisters.

stand. ²⁵ And if a house is divided against itself, that house cannot stand. ²⁶ And if Satan has risen up against himself and is divided, he cannot stand but is finished."

Jesus proves that their charge of blasphemy makes no sense at all. He calls on them to repent, and he promises to forgive everyone who blasphemes him — but he warns them not to blaspheme the Holy Spirit. Jesus says:

<u>Verses 28-29</u>: *²⁸ "Amen I tell you: Everything will be forgiven people, their sins and whatever blasphemies they may speak. ²⁹ But whoever blasphemes against the Holy Spirit will never have forgiveness, but is guilty of an eternal sin."*

With these words Jesus also calls on <u>us</u> to repent — to repent for every time we have neglected or even despised the way the Holy Spirit works to create and sustain saving faith in the hearts of sinners. That is the Gospel in his holy Word and the Gospel in his holy Sacraments, for:

- ☞ it is <u>only</u> through these means that the Holy Spirit gives his forgiving grace;

- ☞ it is <u>only</u> through these means that the Holy Spirit keeps us in the one true faith;

- ☞ it is <u>only</u> through these means that the Holy Spirit forgives our sins, no matter how wicked we have been — even forgiving the sin of blasphemy against Jesus himself; and

- ☞ it is <u>only</u> through these means that the Holy Spirit gives eternal life and salvation.

Persistently rejecting the Holy Spirit's "Means of Grace," the Gospel in God's Word and Sacraments, is committing blasphemy against the Holy Spirit. Jesus teaches us here that this is the one and only unforgivable sin.

This is a dire warning for those scribes and for every member of Family #2. It is also a dire warning for his own Family #1. In fact, it is a dire warning for <u>us</u> even today. Do <u>not</u> blaspheme the Holy Spirit by despising God's holy Word and Sacraments! On the contrary, make sure that you are a member of:

Family #3:

<u>This</u> is Jesus' <u>true</u> family — his disciples, his faithful people who regularly sit at his feet for instruction in God's Word and who strive to put his teachings into practice.

<u>Verses 34-35</u>: *³⁴ [Jesus] looked at those who sat around him in a circle and he said, "Look, my mother and my brothers! ³⁵ For whoever does the will of God is my brother and sister and mother."*

How did those people sitting at Jesus' feet become members of his family — his mother and brothers and sisters? They were not born into his Family #3. In fact, they were born already separated from Christ because of their sinful nature. But Jesus called them to sit at his feet. As they listened to his teachings, the Holy Spirit worked faith in their hearts. They came to believe his Words, and now they work hard to put it into practice in their lives. In short, God made them his disciples — Jesus' <u>true</u> family.

How did you and I become part of Jesus' true family? We were <u>not</u> born into it, either. On the contrary! What we inherited from our parents is <u>genetic death</u>! As Jesus told Nicodemus: *"Whatever is born of the flesh is flesh. Whatever is born of the Spirit is spirit."*[2] We were already separated from God by our sinful nature when we were conceived in our mothers' wombs, but our Heavenly Father adopted us into his holy family simply because he is merciful and loving. God wants us to spend eternity with him, so he chose us out of the "orphanage" of this sin-filled world to be his holy saints!

In the waters of Baptism God *"gave us a new birth into a living hope through the resurrection of Jesus Christ from the dead."*[3] Through this Sacrament the Holy Spirit moved into our souls and kicked out Satan and his minions. Through this Sacrament the Spirit began motivating us to love and obey our Heavenly Father and our dear Redeemer Jesus. He washed us with his blood, he cleansed us from our sins, and he continues to teach us God's holy will on the pages of the Bible.

---

[2] John 3:6

[3] 1 Peter 1:3

What great blessings we have as members of Jesus' family!

- ☞ He rescued us from Satan's family and from eternal damnation.
- ☞ He saved us to receive God's love every day (no matter how badly our day is going).
- ☞ He saved us to experience Christian love and encouragement with fellow members of Jesus' family, and to enjoy the fellowship of like-minded believers.

Such great blessings to be members of Jesus' family! How shall we respond? How shall we show our appreciation and love for the Head of our family who adopted us? Jesus tells us how. He says: *"If you love me, hold on to my commands."*[4] Obedience to God's Word shows our love for him who loved us and gave his life for us. Obedience to Jesus' teachings proves that we really are members of his dear family, as he says in the last verse of our text: *"Whoever does the will of God is my brother and sister and mother."*

Yes, family ties are very important. Each of us was born into a unique family, and we were raised from infancy to adulthood in our own family. Think of the countless times that we get together as families to celebrate birthdays, baptisms, confirmations, graduations, weddings, and anniversaries. As time goes on it seems that, more often than not, our families get together for occasional reunions and then funerals — but it's still family.

It's often said that blood is thicker than water — but Jesus' blood is <u>much</u> thicker yet! Remember: *"The blood of Jesus Christ, [God's] Son, cleanses us from all sin."*[5] So it is much more important to be a member of <u>Jesus'</u> family than any other family in the world. In fact, it is of <u>eternal</u> importance!

Do you want to attend the never ending family reunion at the home of your Creator? You cannot seek him out and find him on your own terms. So much for the deists; that's what <u>they</u> want to do. But no sinner can seek and find God. That's not how it works. God is hidden from sinners. Instead, <u>this</u> is how God works:

---

[4] John 14:15

[5] 1 John 1:7

- ☞ <u>He</u> comes to <u>you</u> in his still, small voice which is found only in the Holy Scriptures;
- ☞ <u>He</u> comes to <u>you</u> through the waters of Holy Baptism; and
- ☞ <u>He</u> comes to <u>you</u> through the body and blood of his Son Jesus in the Lord's Supper.

Through these Means of Grace, God comes to you and makes you a member of his family, blesses you as his own dear child, and preserves you safe in his household for time and eternity. AMEN.

The 4th Sunday after Pentecost

TEXT: Mark 4:26-34

²⁶ Jesus said, "The kingdom of God is like this: A man scatters seed on the ground, ²⁷ and while he sleeps and rises, night and day, the seed sprouts and grows, though he does not know how. ²⁸ The ground produces fruit on its own: first the blade, then the head, then the full grain in the head. ²⁹ When the crop is ready, he swings the sickle without delay, because the harvest has come."

³⁰ Then he said, "To what should we compare the kingdom of God? Or with what parable may we picture it? ³¹ It is like a mustard seed, which when sown on the ground is one of the smallest of all the seeds planted in the ground. ³² Yet when it is planted, it grows up and becomes larger than all the garden plants and puts out large branches so that the birds of the sky can nest under its shade."

³³ With many similar parables he continued to speak the word to them, as much as they were able to hear. ³⁴ He did not speak to them without a parable. But when he was alone with his disciples, he explained everything to them. ✠

The Gospel of our Lord. Praise be to you, O Christ!

In the name of Jesus, dear Christian friends:

We all had many teachers in our lives — especially during our school days. Some of them we thought were wonderful teachers. Others we thought were not so good. The ability to teach is to a large degree an inborn talent. Some connect very well with students, while others don't seem to be able to communicate their lessons very well at all, regardless of how much education they have.

Most professional educators and psychologists say that Jesus of Nazareth was an outstanding teacher — whether or not they agree with him. When it comes to a teacher getting his point across, Jesus was certainly the greatest teacher ever!

Now Jesus was not using the words of our Gospel lesson to motivate anybody to do anything. He was simply teaching his disciples some very important concepts which they needed to know and understand. It's just as important for us to know and understand these truths today as it was back then! In our Gospel lesson,

Jesus Teaches Us about the Kingdom of God

Gathered along the shore of the Sea of Galilee, Jesus taught his disciples some very important lessons about the nature of God's Kingdom. At that time there were many erroneous ideas about the Kingdom of God being spread around. One of the most popular ideas taught in the synagogues was that someday God would send his Messiah to lead all of the Jews in revolt, kicking the Roman soldiers out of the Holy Land, and setting up his rule with Jerusalem as his capital city, where he would reign over all of God's people for a thousand years.

Sadly, this Jewish notion is still being taught and believed by many millions of well-intentioned Christians even to this day. It's called "millennialism." Many Christians wrongly believe that Jesus is going to return from heaven to set up a thousand year reign over the kingdoms of this world with Jerusalem as his capital. For this reason they strongly support the modern nation of Israel, because they believe that the Jewish state today is the fulfilment of biblical prophecy. This way of thinking is called "Zionism."

But this is nothing new! Misunderstandings about the nature of God's Kingdom have been around for thousands of years, so Jesus went about setting the record straight. Many of his closest disciples were still holding on to that ancient heresy when Jesus ascended into heaven. They asked him: *"Lord, is this the time when you are going to restore the kingdom to Israel?"*[1] Rather than chewing them out for being so dense — for still not understanding the lessons he had taught them — Jesus simply responded:

<u>Acts 1:7-8</u>: *⁷It is not for you to know the times or seasons that*

---

[1] Acts 1:6

the Father has set by his own authority. ⁸ But you will receive power when the Holy Spirit has come upon you, and you will be my witnesses in Jerusalem, in all Judea and Samaria, and to the ends of the earth.

For over three years Jesus had repeatedly taught his disciples about the nature of God's Kingdom, yet they still didn't get it. They were still looking forward to an earthly kingdom — one with palaces and armies and bureaucrats and policies both foreign and domestic — with borders you can plot on a map. Jesus taught his disciples again and again that his was not an earthly kingdom, but a spiritual one. In fact, Jesus spent far more time and effort teaching them about the nature of the God's Kingdom than about any other topic! Recall his words to Pontius Pilate:

"My kingdom is not of this world. If my kingdom were of this world, my servants would fight so that I would not be handed over to the Jews. But now my kingdom is not from here."

"You are a king then?" Pilate asked. Jesus answered, "I am, as you say, a king. For this reason I was born, and for this reason I came into the world, to testify to the truth. Everyone who belongs to the truth listens to my voice."[2]

Pontius Pilate quickly understood that Jesus was not claiming to be the king of any physical, worldly kingdom, but of a spiritual kingdom *"not of this world."* Pilate repeatedly referred to Jesus as *"the King of the Jews"*[3] — and Pilate was correct, though he didn't go far enough. Jesus <u>was</u> and <u>is</u> the King of kings and the Lord of lords — King of the Jews and King of us Gentiles as well!

In our sermon text today Jesus used <u>two</u> parables to teach his people about the Kingdom of God. He often used simple, concrete illustrations to teach very important abstract truths. And that's what a parable is. It's <u>not</u> an earthly story with a heavenly meaning. A parable is an illustration, an extended metaphor, which uses some picture from everyday life or some easily imaginable story. This is an excellent teaching method, leading students from the simple to the

---

[2] John 18:36-37

[3] Matthew 27:11,37; Mark 15:2,9,12,26; Luke 23:3,38; John 18:33,39; 19:19

complex, from the known to the unknown, from the concrete to the abstract. Yes, Jesus did come into this world to establish his Kingdom — which is an abstract concept for simple sinners to grasp. Yet it's vitally important for his followers to understand what he was all about, what he was doing, and what he was setting out to accomplish. So in this portion of God's Word Jesus uses two parables to teach them — and to teach us — about the nature of God's Kingdom. First, he teaches:

Part 1: The Parable of the Growing Seed

Verses 26-29: *²⁶ Jesus said, "The kingdom of God is like this: A man scatters seed on the ground, ²⁷ and while he sleeps and rises, night and day, the seed sprouts and grows, though he does not know how. ²⁸ The ground produces fruit on its own: first the blade, then the head, then the full grain in the head. ²⁹ When the crop is ready, he swings the sickle without delay, because the harvest has come."*

The farmer simply sows the seed. He does nothing to make it grow. He doesn't even know how it grows, really. It just grows — whether the man is awake or asleep. All by itself, so it seems, the planted seed grows and the field produces grain. Then the combine comes through the field to harvest the crop.

Wow! So that's what the Kingdom of God is like. Did you get it? Jesus' disciples didn't.

The seed, you see, is God's Word. And the point of comparison? Just as the seed seems to have some mysterious power to sprout and grow and produce a crop, so God's Word has the mysterious power to sprout and grow and produce a crop. The seed works. It grows. You can't see it happening, but it does what it does. It grows up and produces a crop.

God's Word also works. The seed produces whatever kind of harvest God wants it to produce. So it is with God's Word! It produces many good fruits in the hearts and lives of God's people. God's Word produces an abundant harvest of souls for God, at just the right time and in the exact measure God wills, just as the seed produces a crop in the field.

The man who plants the seed has nothing to do with the power that gives it growth. That's God's business. The farmer can hinder the seed's growth by failing to plant the seed in the first place, or by fertilizing it incorrectly, or by failing to irrigate it properly if the soil is too dry, but the farmer cannot <u>cause</u> the seed to sprout and grow and produce a crop. That's <u>God's</u> job. Neither the one who sows the seed, nor the one in whom the seed is planted, is responsible for its growth. That's <u>God's</u> job.

In this parable Jesus teaches that the power which causes God's Kingdom to grow is <u>God</u>'s power, and God places his power in his holy Word. No human being causes God's kingdom to grow! That's God's job. Our job is that of the farmer. We are charged by God to spread the seed of his Word — and to trust in the Lord for the harvest.

Jesus went on to teach more about the nature of God's Kingdom, using another parable:

Part 2: The Parable of the Mustard Seed.

<u>Verses 30-32</u>: *³⁰ Jesus said, "To what should we compare the kingdom of God? Or with what parable may we picture it? ³¹ It is like a mustard seed, which when sown on the ground is one of the smallest of all the seeds planted in the ground. ³² Yet when it is planted, it grows up and becomes larger than all the garden plants and puts out large branches so that the birds of the sky can nest under its shade."*

Mustard is the smallest seed that the farmers planted in Jesus' day. Yet the mustard seed grew up to be one of the biggest plants on the farm. The rest of the garden was dwarfed by the mustard plants which made great habitat for birds.

The point of this parable is that the Word of God may seem very small and insignificant, but God uses that small seed of his Word to grow a huge Kingdom — his Holy Christian Church, his Communion of Saints, his Kingdom of Grace and Glory. And God uses that seed — his almighty Word — to produce a bumper crop of blessings for his people.

One reason Jesus taught these parables was to straighten out the terrible misunderstandings that so many people have about the nature of God's Kingdom. What is God's Kingdom? You won't find it on any map or globe. It is God's ruling activity in the hearts and minds and lives of his people through his holy Word. The citizens of God's Kingdom are all those in whom God is ruling as King through his Word. St. Luke tells us that:

Luke 17:20-21: *The Pharisees asked Jesus when the kingdom of God would come. Jesus answered them, "The kingdom of God is not coming in a way you can observe, nor will people say, 'Look, here it is!' or 'Look, there it is!' because the kingdom of God is within you."*

God's kingdom is invisible. It's not to be identified with any visible church, nor with any denomination or church body, nor with any visible organization or congregation, and not with any building or government or nation. Jesus said that *"The kingdom of God is not coming in a way you can observe."* God's Kingdom is his ruling activity in the souls and minds and lives of his people through his holy Word. Jesus says: *"The kingdom of God is within you."*

The Kingdom of God is in the hearts and souls and minds of all people everywhere who repent of their sins and who believe the Good News of salvation through the life, death, and resurrection of Jesus. The citizens of God's Kingdom are all those who trust in Jesus for forgiveness and eternal life. He gave us Holy Baptism to mark us as citizens of his Kingdom and to bless us as his special people in this world and in the next. We don't fall out of God's Kingdom when we die; we are simply moved to a different address where we will dwell in the house of the Lord forever — the heavenly mansion above which Jesus is preparing for us right now.

Another reason why Jesus taught these parables about the nature of God's Kingdom was to address the defeatist attitude his followers often have, thinking such thoughts as these: As long as the Roman soldiers are here and as long as we have to keep paying taxes to Caesar:

- We will never have any freedom; or
- We will never have a decent way of life; or

- ☞ Our kids will never stay faithful to the Lord; or
- ☞ We will never enjoy the prosperity which the prophets promised us.

Those are the kinds of defeatist thoughts which so many Jews had at the time of Christ. In our day we tend to have different thoughts and concerns, but they are produced by the same devil who fills our heads with the same defeatist attitudes which the Jews had in Jesus' day — thoughts such as: Our church will never grow, because:

- ☞ We're in a terrible location; or
- ☞ Our pastor is a poor preacher — or a poor people person; or
- ☞ We're stuck with that old-fashioned liturgy and music; or
- ☞ We've got to change our doctrine and practice in order to keep our young people.

All such ideas are delusions of the devil, and we must recognize them as such!

Brothers and Sisters in Christ, <u>we</u> don't make God's church grow! You don't, and neither do I. Pastors don't cause God's church to grow, either. Only <u>God</u> does that — and only God can! Believing that <u>we</u> are responsible for the growth of God's Kingdom is the sin of arrogance. Yet Jesus died to pay for <u>that</u> sin, too, and he rose again to declare us forgiven.

These are important lessons to learn from Jesus! They are important enough that our Lord felt the need to put them into parables for his people. They're easy for us to learn that way, and they're easy to remember:

- ☞ God's Kingdom is like growing seed. It seems to grow all by itself. <u>We</u> aren't the ones who make it grow — that's God's job. We just sow and reap, plant and harvest, trusting in the Lord to provide the increase!
- ☞ And God's Kingdom is like a mustard seed. It may <u>seem</u> to be tiny and insignificant, but it grows and

grows to become the biggest plant in the garden, and when fully grown it provides wonderful blessings!

So stay faithful to that seemingly insignificant seed of God's Word! Keep on trusting our Lord to provide his growth, when and where and in whatever measure he wills. There's nothing that you or I or anyone else can do to cause God's Kingdom to grow. Just keep on faithfully planting and harvesting, sowing and reaping, trusting the Lord to provide the increase — spreading God's Holy Word, and bringing into his Church all whom the Spirit leads into our midst. AMEN.

The 5th Sunday after Pentecost

TEXT: Mark 4:35-41

³⁵ On that day, when evening came, Jesus said to them, "Let's go over to the other side."

³⁶ After leaving the crowd behind, the disciples took him along in the boat, just as he was. Other small boats also followed him. ³⁷ A great windstorm arose, and the waves were splashing into the boat, so that the boat was quickly filling up. ³⁸ Jesus himself was in the stern, sleeping on a cushion. They woke him and said, "Teacher, don't you care that we are about to drown?"

³⁹ Then he got up, rebuked the wind, and said to the sea, "Peace! Be still!" The wind stopped, and there was a great calm.

⁴⁰ He said to them, "Why are you so afraid? Do you still lack faith?"

⁴¹ They were filled with awe and said to one another, "Who then is this? Even the wind and the sea obey him!" ✠

The Gospel of our Lord. Praise be to you, O Christ!

In Christ Jesus, the almighty Son of God, dear friends:

In 1986 two young Jewish fishermen were walking along the muddy western shore of the Sea of Galilee near Migdal, the modern name of the ancient city of Magdala, home of Mary Magdalene. A serious drought had caused the water level to drop much lower than normal, so certain things which for many years had been submerged were now exposed. One of those fishermen kicked what he thought was a piece of driftwood, but it did not budge. He and his brother tried to dig up that piece of wood, but it got bigger and bigger. It gradually became obvious that they had stumbled upon something of archaeological importance, so they reported their discovery to the authorities who sent out a team of experts to investigate.

THE PENTECOST SEASON

After more digging they discovered that they had stumbled upon the remains of an ancient boat. A secret dig followed, undertaken by members of Kibbutz Ginosar, the Israel Antiquities Authority, and numerous volunteers. Excavating the boat from the mud without damaging it was a difficult process lasting twelve days and nights. Once uncovered from the mud, the boat was submerged in a chemical bath for seven years before it could be displayed at the Yigal Allon Museum in Kibbutz Ginosar. This so-called "Jesus boat" is of tremendous historical importance to Jews and Christians alike since it's the only boat ever discovered dating from the time of Christ. Boats such as this played a large role in Jesus' life and ministry, and they are mentioned fifty times in the four Gospels.

Our sermon text today records for us an event which happened on the Sea of Galilee. That's about 700 feet below sea level; an average depth of 84 feet; eight miles from east to west, and 21 miles from north to south. Jesus and his disciples had boarded several boats, almost certainly boats just like that "Jesus boat" now displayed in its own museum. Then suddenly,

Verses 37-38: *A great windstorm arose, and the waves were splashing into the boat, so that the boat was quickly filling up. Jesus himself was in the stern, sleeping on a cushion. They woke him and said, "Teacher, don't you care that we are about to drown?"*

Sudden squalls on the Sea of Galilee were not uncommon. Its geography is such that you can be sitting in a boat in the middle of the calm lake under clear skies, when suddenly — within just a few minutes — the wind can pick up, ominous clouds fill the sky, and waves begin breaking over the gunnels.

One day, while Jesus and his disciples were sailing across the Sea of Galilee, they learned an amazing lesson:

Even the Wind and the Sea Obey Jesus!

The sudden storm was bad enough to scare his disciples, at least half of whom had grown up on that body of water as professional fishermen. Even they were so terrified that they woke up their sleeping Savior and asked him:

Part 1: "Teacher, Don't You Care That We Are about to Drown?"

Now was that question an act of a <u>strong</u> faith, or of <u>weak</u> faith, or of <u>no</u> faith at all?

His disciples were filled with fear. This same Jesus, who had told them repeatedly that he is God's Son and their Savior, had not yet offered himself as the sacrifice for their sins. Shouldn't they have trusted in the fact that nothing — surely not this storm! — was going to prevent Jesus from keeping his promises and carrying out his saving work?

<u>Verses 39-41</u>: *³⁹ Then [Jesus] got up, rebuked the wind, and said to the sea, "Peace! Be still!" The wind stopped, and there was a great calm.*

⁴⁰ He said to [his disciples], "Why are you so afraid? Do you still lack faith?"

⁴¹ They were filled with awe and said to one another, "Who then is this? Even the wind and the sea obey him!"

Only the law-giver can set aside the laws which he has established. Only God, the Creator of all things, can set aside the laws of nature which he established at creation. And since Jesus did exactly that — since Jesus set aside the laws of nature by stilling the storm by the power of his own Word — Jesus must be the law-giver. He must be the Creator. For God is the One who established the laws of nature at creation, and Jesus temporarily set them aside when he stilled the storm. Jesus must be God!

But did this miracle immediately convince Jesus' disciples? When he asked them *"Why are you so afraid? Do you still lack faith?"* They were filled with awe and said to one another, *"Who then is this? Even the wind and the sea obey him!"*

Part 2: Yes, Even the Wind and the Sea <u>Do</u> Obey Him!

After all:

- ☞ This is Jesus, the Christ, the Son of the living God.
- ☞ This is Jesus, the same Divine Being who caused the wind to blow and the waves to toss St. Paul's ship on

The Pentecost Season

the Mediterranean Sea, led that ship to the island of Malta, and caused it to break into pieces when it ran aground on the rocky shore.[1]

- ☞ This is Jesus, the same Divine Being who miraculously preserved the lives of Paul and Luke and everyone else aboard that ship.[2]

- ☞ This is Jesus, the same Creator who established all the laws of physics and chemistry and biology and mathematics when he said *"Let there be..."* and there was! — and in six days he called this entire creation into existence with his all-powerful Word.[3]

So yes, even the wind and the waves <u>do</u> obey him!

What's amazing is that this God-in-human-flesh, this God-man Jesus, cares about us sinners so much that he preserves our lives. He protects us from so much harm and danger. He even rescues our souls from the devil himself. True God from all eternity, Jesus became a man, born of the virgin Mary, and lived under his own laws which he had established in the first place. In Jesus of Nazareth, God <u>did</u> walk a mile in our moccasins, as it were.

And yet in Jesus of Nazareth God subjected his <u>immortal</u> nature to <u>mortality</u>. The <u>im</u>mortal God became mortal man in order to suffer and die to atone for all of our sins. He willingly went to Calvary's cross and suffered the punishment for our sins which otherwise would have been ours. He suffered the torture of hell itself in order to spare <u>us</u> that punishment. <u>He</u> died that <u>we</u> might live!

No grave could hold Jesus — not even one freshly hewn out of solid limestone, closed shut by a huge stone requiring several men to move, sealed with the governor's own mortar and signet ring, and guarded by a squad of Roman soldiers with orders to kill any of their fellow guards if any one of them would dare to doze off on guard duty. Yet two days after his burial, Jesus rose back to life from the

---

[1] Acts 27:14-41

[2] Acts 27:42–28:9

[3] Genesis 1 and 2, *passim*; Exodus 20:11; John 1:1-3

dead! An angel rolled away the stone to reveal that Jesus' tomb was already empty. Jesus had defeated death and the grave!

But that really ought not surprise us. After all, Jesus is true God in human flesh. He established the laws of nature, and every one of his miracles proved his ability to manipulate those laws. As true God and true man in one person, Jesus can even rise back to life from the dead — and he did! And when he commands the bad weather: *"Peace! Be still!"* should it surprise us that *"Even the wind and the sea obey him"*? So when Jesus says *"Take heart, son! Your sins are forgiven!"*[4] you can believe that, too! AMEN.

---

[4] Matthew 9:2

THE PENTECOST SEASON

The 6th Sunday after Pentecost

TEXT: Lamentations 3:22-33

²² By the mercies of the LORD we are not consumed,
   for his compassions do not fail.
²³ They are new every morning.
   Great is your faithfulness.
²⁴ My soul says, "The LORD is my portion.
   Therefore, I will hope in him."
²⁵ The LORD is good to those who wait for him,
   to the soul who seeks him.
²⁶ It is good to hope quietly for the salvation of the LORD.
²⁷ It is good for a man that he bears a yoke early in his life.
²⁸ Let him sit alone and be silent,
   Because the LORD has laid this upon him.
²⁹ Let him stick his face in the dust.
   Perhaps there still is hope.
³⁰ Let him turn his cheek toward the one who strikes him.
   Let him be filled with disgrace.
³¹ For the LORD will not push us away forever.
³² Even though he brings grief,
   he will show compassion on the basis of his great mercy.
³³ Certainly it is not what his heart desires when he causes affliction,
   when he brings grief to the children of men. ✡

The Word of our LORD. Thanks be to God!

In the name of our merciful Lord Jesus, dear friends:

Imagine this: Rather than the United States and our allies sending troops into Iraq, just imagine that Saddam Hussein had invaded <u>your</u> state instead. You heard about it in the news: Saddam is coming with his army, marching into your dear home town and the neighboring villages, bombing and shelling and looting and raping and pillaging and burning, capturing every healthy man, woman, and child, dragging them away and shipping them off to Baghdad.

Now you are sitting on one of the hills overlooking your home town and neighborhood from a relatively safe distance, with a vista of your old stomping grounds, watching your community and your home and your church being pillaged and burned to the ground — the only place where you have worshipped God all your life, the place where you were baptized and confirmed and married, where your parents and grandparents were, too, and where your children and grandchildren were as well. So much for your desire to have your funeral someday at your own home church!

Your heart would be filled with sorrow, and you would <u>lament</u> the crimes you were witnessing. If you were to write down what you were seeing and thinking — if you were to write down the pain you're experiencing in your heart — you would have a book containing your <u>lamentations</u>.

That's what Jeremiah saw, and that's exactly what he did. Nebuchadnezzar, the wicked king of Babylon, came to Jerusalem with his Babylonian troops in 586 B.C. They came raping and pillaging, destroying and burning, leveling Jerusalem and the LORD's temple, and carrying off to Babylon 90% of God's people who survived the battle. Jeremiah watched the destruction and devastation from a hill outside the city, and as he watched, he lamented the things he witnessed.

Why? Why, O LORD, do you allow such atrocities? Why do you permit these heathen soldiers to destroy your holy temple and your holy city and your chosen people?

But Jeremiah knew why. He knew the answers to his rhetorical questions. This was the consequence of everything he had spent his entire life preaching to these people. His message had been this: If you remain wicked, persistently and consistently turning your backs on the LORD and his covenant, the LORD will eventually turn his back on <u>you</u> and allow you to be taken off into captivity. He will allow the Babylonians to destroy Jerusalem and even the LORD's own temple.

But sadly, God's people did not heed his prophet's message. The people of Judah had been thoroughly <u>un</u>faithful to the LORD who had been so very merciful and patient and faithful to them. So at long last, after many centuries of putting up with their unfaithfulness, God raised up the Babylonian army to destroy Jerusalem and to deport most of the survivors back to the land from which their ancestor Abraham had come — back to Babylonia.

In spite of the disaster Jeremiah witnessed with his own eyes, he still trusted in his heart that God would keep his promises. God had promised to send his Son to save the world, and he had promised to send his Son into this world through the tribe of Judah — but he had not yet done so. But rather than despairing, rather than cursing God, rather than giving up his faith and trust and hope in the LORD, Jeremiah lamented through his tears:

Verses 22-24 — *²² By the mercies of the LORD we are not consumed, for his compassions do not fail.*
²³ They are new every morning. Great is your faithfulness.
²⁴ My soul says, "The LORD is my portion. Therefore, I will hope in him."

Jeremiah still trusted that God would keep his promises. Why? Because, as he said:

Great is God's Faithfulness!

Part 1: God Is Faithful to the People He Takes as His Own.

About 2,000 years before Christ, God chose Abram of Chaldean Ur to be patriarch of his special people — not because of anything special about Abram, but simply because God wanted to make Abram his own. God freely chose to bind himself to Abram and to his descendants by making a solemn covenant of grace with them. These are the three covenant promises God made:

1) Abram and his descendants would someday inherit the Land of Canaan;

2) His descendants would be as numerous as the stars in the sky and as the grains of sand on the seashore; and

3) The Messiah, the Christ, the only-begotten Son of God, would be one of Abram's descendants. Through him all the nations of the earth would be blessed.

A thousand years later, the LORD God promised King David that one of <u>his</u> descendants would reign on his throne <u>forever</u>.

But now in 586 B.C. the Babylonians were in the process of destroying the nation of Judah, destroying God's covenant people, his holy city, and even his holy temple — the only place on earth where God permitted sacrifices to be made to atone for sins. Heathen forces were taking God's people away from their Promised Land. But God had <u>bound</u> himself to them! Abraham had believed God's promises. St. Paul says that *"Abraham believed God and it was credited to him as righteousness."*[1]

Dear brothers and sisters, simply because God is gracious and merciful, he has also chosen you and me — sinners though we are — to be his own beloved children forever. From all eternity, even before he created this world, God chose us to be his own special people, and he determined to rescue us from eternal damnation.

So at just the right moment in history, when God had led the affairs of mankind to just the right point, he sent his Son Jesus into this world. He entered his world through the womb of a virgin named Mary of Nazareth. He grew up to be a famous rabbi and teacher of God's Word. He proved his divine authority by performing countless miracles, demonstrating his love for fallen mankind. Though he never committed even a single sin, he suffered the punishment that <u>we</u> all deserve for <u>our</u> many sins. He died on a Roman cross as God's sacrificial Lamb in order to pay for the sins of the whole world. Two days later he rose back to life from the dead and declared his victory over sin, over death, and over the power of the devil — and he did it all <u>for us</u>!

The risen Christ promises eternal salvation to everyone who trusts in his saving work and receives Holy Baptism in the name of the Triune God. As our risen Redeemer says: *"Whoever believes and is baptized will be saved, but whoever does not believe will be condemned."*[2] And you can take that promise to the bank, because **God is faithful to the people he takes as his own**, and:

---

[1] Romans 4:3; which is quoted in Galatians 3:6 and James 2:23
[2] Mark 16:16

Part 2: God Is Faithful to the Promises He Makes to His Own.

Our LORD made those promises to Abram and to his descendants. Jeremiah was a descendent of Abram, and he trusted God to keep those promises! Jeremiah's hope was in the LORD. He knew it was best to wait on the LORD to keep his promises because God always comes through at just the right time. He says in:

<u>Verses 25-27</u>: *²⁵ The LORD is good to those who wait for him, to the soul who seeks him.*
²⁶ It is good to hope quietly for the salvation of the LORD.
²⁷ It is good for a man that he bears a yoke early in his life.

Jeremiah was confident that, when the people repented of their sins, God would forgive them, show them compassion, and deliver them from their enemies. He says in:

<u>Verses 28-33</u>: *²⁸ Let him sit alone and be silent, because the LORD has laid this upon him.*
²⁹ Let him stick his face in the dust. Perhaps there still is hope.
³⁰ Let him turn his cheek toward the one who strikes him. Let him be filled with disgrace.
³¹ For the LORD will not push us away forever.
³² Even though he brings grief, he will show compassion on the basis of his great mercy.
³³ Certainly it is not what his heart desires when he causes affliction, when he brings grief to the children of men.

You see, God is always faithful to the promises he has made! He will never forget his beloved children. God will never leave us nor forsake us. He will always feed us, clothe us, and provide us with shelter. God will always defend and protect his people from the devil and from his evil demons. God will always forgive us our sins and comfort us when our hearts are filled with grief and sorrow. God will always be here to guard us and guide us though every hardship and adversity.

But back to Jeremiah. Seventy years later God <u>did</u> deliver his people from captivity in Babylonia, just as he had promised. And

God still _did_ keep _all three_ of those great promises he had made to Abram and to his descendants:

1) The Holy Land of Canaan _did_ become theirs;

2) Abram's descendants _are_ as numberless as the stars in the sky and as the grains of sand on the seashore; and

3) The Messiah, God's only-begotten Son Jesus, _did_ come into this world, and he rescued us from sin, from death, and from the power of the devil — not with gold or silver, but with his holy, precious blood, and with his innocent suffering and death.

On the third day after his crucifixion, Jesus rose back to life from the dead in order to reign on David's throne forever, just as God had promised.

Remember: God _always_ keeps his Word. He never forgets his people. You can trust in everything he says! Our Lord has a perfect track record of keeping his promises, and he will surely keep every one of his promises to us, too. Someday Jesus will return to take us to be with him at the right hand of our Heavenly Father — just as he promised.

So let us say with Jeremiah, **"*Great Is Your Faithfulness, O Lord!*"** God is always faithful to his people! And God always keeps his promises, for he never fails to keep his Word. AMEN.

The 7ᵗʰ Sunday after Pentecost

TEXT: 2 Corinthians 12:7-10

⁷ To keep me from becoming arrogant due to the extraordinary nature of these revelations, I was given a thorn in my flesh, a messenger of Satan, to torment me, so that I would not become arrogant. ⁸ Three times I pleaded with the Lord about this, that he would take it away from me. ⁹ And he said to me, "My grace is sufficient for you, because my power is made perfect in weakness." Therefore I will be glad to boast all the more in my weaknesses, so that the power of Christ may shelter me.

¹⁰ That is why I delight in weaknesses, in insults, in hardships, in persecutions, in difficulties, for the sake of Christ. For whenever I am weak, then am I strong. ✠

The Word of the Lord. Thanks be to God!

In the name of our Great Physician Jesus, dear friends:

You may recall the ancient story about the big, ferocious lion who got a thorn stuck in his paw. He growled and roared and then he growled and roared some more. All the other animals in the jungle were terrified because the king of the jungle was so loud and angry! No other animal had the courage to approach that miserable lion — until finally a little mouse did. He walked up to that lion and pulled that nasty thorn out of his paw. Instantly the king of the jungle was relieved of his pain. He was so thrilled about his pain relief that, rather than eating that daring little mouse, the lion cozied up to him and made him his best buddy in the whole world!

Now that is an ancient Greek fable by Aesop. St. Paul had been educated in the Greek schools of ancient Tarsus in southeastern Turkey, so he knew the story about the mouse and the thorn in the lion's flesh. This is where Paul got that figure of speech, for he had a thorn in his <u>own</u> flesh, too. So do we all! We may be tempted to ask God, "Why do you leave me to suffer with this thorn in my flesh?" We may even be tempted, as was the prophet Job about 4,000 years ago, to accuse God of being unjust, unloving, unfair, or not even really being there for us at all. It's at times like these that we need to learn this important lesson that God taught St. Paul, and that Paul, in turn, teaches us:

The Thorns in Our Flesh Keep Us Strong!

Paul was not born a saint. He was not even born Paul! He was born Saul of Tarsus, a Jew from a big Gentile city in what is today southeastern Turkey. When he grew up he went off to Jerusalem to study under the famous rabbi Gamaliel. Saul became a lawyer and a theologian. He describes himself as a Pharisee among Pharisees. He made it his business to try to stamp out Christianity by persecuting and stamping out Christians.

One day, while leading an entourage to Damascus, Syria, intending to arrest the Christians there and to drag them back to Jerusalem, Saul was confronted by our risen Savior Jesus! The Lord appeared to Saul from heaven. The shock of this vision knocked him to the ground. Jesus spoke to him: *"Saul, Saul, why are you persecuting me? You're fighting a losing battle!"*

"Who are you, Lord?" Saul asked — knowing full well that it was the Lord Jesus himself.

"I am Jesus, whom you are persecuting," he said. *"Now get up and go ahead into Damascus, and there I will tell you what you need to do."*[1]

A minister in Damascus named Ananias baptized Saul and introduced him to the congregation of Christians. All of a sudden, the man who used to persecute Christians began to preach salvation through faith alone in Jesus! Saul preached that Jesus was the Messiah for whom God's people had been waiting for so many centuries. When the Jews got wind of this, they went after Saul to kill him. So the Christians helped Saul escape by using ropes to lower him in a basket through a hole in the city wall.[2]

---

[1] Cf. Acts 9:1-6, 22:3-16, and 26:9-18. In Galatians 1:11-24 Paul discusses what happened after his conversion.

[2] Acts 9:7-23

From there God led Saul out into the Arabian desert where he lived as a hermit for the next three years. During that time Jesus appeared to him from heaven in a series of visions, and he instructed Saul in the details of the Gospel. All of the other apostles had received three years of training at Jesus' feet before he suffered and died for the sins of the world, rose back to life, commissioned his Church to gather disciples from every nation, and then ascended back into heaven. But Saul received his three years of training by Jesus through that series of visions he received while living in the Arabian desert.[3]

Years later, God called Saul to be his apostle to the Gentiles and to take the Good News of Jesus to the people of modern day Cyprus and Turkey, Macedonia and Greece, Caesarea and Malta, and even to Rome. God used the former persecutor Saul, whose name was changed to Paul, to proclaim the Gospel even before kings![4]

How easy it might have been for him to become conceited! God took Saul and made a saint out of him, and God made him to be the greatest Christian missionary ever! How could Christ's Church get along without all the ministry Paul did? He was tutored personally by Jesus himself, and he became the greatest Christian theologian in history. The Holy Spirit inspired him to write 13 books of the New Testament. Jesus even gave Paul a vision of heaven itself. Jesus gave him the miraculous ability to heal the sick, to exorcize demons from those who were possessed, and to preach the Gospel in foreign languages which he had never studied.

Now, when we read his Second Letter to the Corinthians, we learn that:

Part 1: St. Paul Had a Thorn in His Flesh.

He tells us in:

Verse 7: *To keep me from becoming arrogant due to the extraordinary nature of these revelations, I was given a thorn in my flesh, a messenger of Satan, to torment me, so that I would not become arrogant.*

---

[3] Galatians 1:16^B-17

[4] Acts 13:1-9

Paul says that God gave him that "thorn" in his flesh to keep him from getting too big a head — to keep him from becoming too full of himself and of his own self-importance. God did not want him to become arrogant — which was a real temptation for this great apostle, to be sure!

But Paul never tells us what his "thorn" was! Nobody knows what it was. A bum leg, perhaps? A bad back? A trick knee? Many Bible scholars suggest that, since on two occasions his enemies had tried to kill him by stoning him and leaving him for dead, Paul may have had an eye put out by one of those stones, or perhaps he was now subject to seizures — either of which scenario would have made many ancient people fearful that Paul might be demon possessed.

But whatever that thorn was, it was a real physical problem which made his missionary travels and work much more difficult. You can almost hear him complain, "Lord, if only you would take away this thorn from my flesh, I could do so much <u>more</u> mission work for you! I could get so much <u>more</u> ministry accomplished. I could reach out to so many <u>more</u> people, and <u>more</u> people might be converted to the faith!"

Yet in his eternal wisdom God did not take that thorn out of Paul's flesh. Instead, God enabled Paul <u>to live with it</u>. It was God's will that Paul should suffer for a little while until the Day when God would give Paul the crown of eternal life in paradise where there are no more thorns and where there is no more suffering.

I'm glad that St. Paul did not tell us exactly <u>what</u> that thorn in his flesh was. This makes it much easier for us to read <u>ourselves</u> into these words of Scripture — that is, to apply these words of God to <u>ourselves</u>. Whatever his thorn was doesn't really matter to us; yet these words apply to you and to me just as well as they applied to Paul, because:

Part 2: You and I Get Thorns in Our Flesh, Too.

What thorns do you have stuck in <u>your</u> flesh? Cardiac problems? Asthma? Cancer? Arthritis? Back pain? Diabetes? Macular degeneration? Hearing loss? Whatever your physical ailments are, those are the thorns in <u>your</u> flesh. The thorns in our flesh are messengers from Satan. His message is this: "God is not listening to your prayers! God does not care about you. Give up your faith in Christ, because he won't help you anyway!"

Then what shall we do about our thorns? God's Word teaches us to pray, pray, and pray — to pray without ceasing. That's what St. Paul did. He says in:

Verses 8-9: *⁸ Three times I pleaded with the Lord about this, that he would take it away from me. ⁹ And he said to me, "My grace is sufficient for you, because my power is made perfect in weakness."*

Apparently God answered Paul's prayers by saying "No!" God did not take away the thorn from his flesh. Instead, God mercifully gave him the strength to endure his weakness.

God never promised to deliver us from all evil. Paul told newly converted Christians in Pisidian Antioch: *"We must go through many troubles on our way to the kingdom of God."*[5] Sometimes God delivers us through the evils we must endure by giving us strength, hope, the comfort of his love, and assurance of final deliverance from all our thorns and pains and suffering when he takes us to heaven. Until then we must continue, with God's help, to struggle with those thorns in our flesh, always confident in the sufficiency of God's grace and power.

But why? Why does God allow Satan to send us these messengers? Why does God permit thorns in our flesh to make us miserable? And why doesn't God always say "Yes!" to our prayers when we beg him for relief from the thorns in our flesh? Why must we endure any thorns at all? St. Paul teaches us that:

Part 3: God Uses Our Thorns to Make Us Strong!

God says to Paul in:

Verses 9-10: *⁹ "My grace is sufficient for you, because my power is made perfect in weakness." Therefore* [Paul says] *I will be glad to boast all the more in my weaknesses, so that the power of Christ may shelter me. ¹⁰ That is why I delight in weaknesses, in insults, in hardships, in persecu-*

---

[5] Acts 14:22

tions, in difficulties, for the sake of Christ. For whenever I am weak, then am I strong.

God's grace was all that Paul really needed, and God's grace is sufficient for <u>us</u>, <u>too</u>, for God's power is made perfect in weakness!

<u>What does this mean</u>? St. Paul explains this to us in that short little sentence in verse 10: *"Whenever I am weak, then am I strong."*

There you go! That's the key to understanding Paul's point: *"Whenever I am weak, then am I strong."* The weaker we are — the more we suffer with the thorns in our flesh — the more we realize just how much we depend on God for every breath we take and every move we make. The weaker that we are, the more we must lean upon the power of Christ to shelter us and to strengthen us. So when we are weak, as Paul says, then we are strong! This seems so counter-intuitive — and yet it's so very true:

The Thorns in Our Flesh Keep Us Strong!

God knows how our sinful pride can pull us away from him. That thorn in Paul's flesh was not just a messenger from Satan. It was also God's tool to keep him humble and to keep him connected to his <u>real</u> source of strength — to his Lord Jesus. And when <u>we</u> are weak, we despair of ourselves and finally lean upon the power of Christ. We entrust our well being and our very lives to Jesus. The weaker we are physically and mentally, the more we <u>need</u> to lean on Jesus for comfort and strength.

Jesus loves us very much. He loves us so much that he willingly sacrificed his life for us! He loves us so much that he lived for us, died for us, rose back to life for us, ascended into heaven to prepare a place for us, and promised that he will someday return for each one of us. Now since God loves us so much, do you think that he will ever forget about us or forsake us? Of course not! Remember:

The Thorns in Our Flesh Keep Us Strong!

They are constant reminders that God's love in Jesus is all that we really need! AMEN.

THE PENTECOST SEASON

The 8th Sunday after Pentecost

TEXT: Amos 7:10-17

¹⁰ Then Amaziah, the priest of Bethel, sent a message to Jeroboam king of Israel:

> Amos has conspired against you in the midst of the house of Israel. The land is not able to endure all of his words. ¹¹ This is what Amos says: "Jeroboam will die by the sword, and Israel will certainly go into exile away from its own soil."

¹² Then Amaziah said to Amos, "You seer, get out of here! Flee to the land of Judah. You may eat food and prophesy there. ¹³ But you must never again prophesy at Bethel, for it is the sanctuary of the king and the national temple."

¹⁴ Then Amos responded to Amaziah:

> I was not a prophet, nor was I a son of a prophet. Rather, I was a sheep breeder and I took care of sycamore fig trees. ¹⁵ But the LORD took me from tending flocks, and the LORD said to me, "Go, prophesy to my people Israel."
>
> ¹⁶ But now, hear the word of the LORD, you who are saying, "Do not prophesy against Israel" and "Do not preach against the house of Isaac."
>
> ¹⁷ This is what the LORD says: "Your wife will be a prostitute in the city, and your sons and your daughters will fall by the sword. Your land will be parceled out with a measuring line, and as for you, you will die upon unclean soil. And Israel will certainly go into exile far away from its own soil." ✡

The Word of the LORD. Thanks be to God!

In Christ Jesus, dear friends:

The Holy Scriptures teach us some very important lessons about preachers who claim to be God's spokesmen:

- ☞ St. Paul teaches St. Timothy [1] what to look for when recruiting, training, and ordaining men to the office of the holy ministry. In a very wicked society, not many men are qualified. Paul spells out specific qualifications for the pastoral office. If you're going to be a spokesman for the Lord, you must fit the position description.

- ☞ Jesus called and then commissioned his apostles to preach, teach, and heal [2]. The Lord called them, he empowered them, he gave them authority to be his own spokesmen, and he gave them his own message to proclaim to his own people.

- ☞ Our Old Testament reading today is our sermon text, written by the prophet Amos. Here we find the great contrast between a preacher of God's truth and righteousness on the one hand, and on the other a preacher of heresy and wickedness. One leads God's people to eternal life; the other leads people to eternal damnation. The contrast cannot be more clear than what we read in chapter 7 about Amos and Amaziah.

As we study the contrast between these to men who claimed to be God's spokesmen, we learn something very important that we must always remember:

God Is Very Serious about His Word!

First of all,

Part 1: What Do We Know about Amos?

He was <u>not</u> trained to be a prophet. That was <u>not</u> his vocational goal. He was a sheep breeder and a fig picker from Tekoa, a village eleven miles south of Jerusalem. Though he was <u>not</u> a professionally

---

[1] 1 Timothy 3:1-7
[2] Mark 6:7-13

trained preacher, the Word of the LORD came to Amos in some way. We're not told how it came to him: in a vision, in a voice, or perhaps in a dream? Did God assume human form and speak to Amos, as he had when he spoke to Abraham and Jacob and Samuel? Did God send an angel to Amos? We don't know. The book of Amos repeatedly says: "... *thus says the LORD....*" What we can say with certainty is that the Holy Spirit inspired the words which Amos preached to his people and which he wrote down as the Word of God.

Amos lived and worked about 750 years before Christ, during the ministries of the prophets Isaiah and Hosea, during the days of the divided kingdom, while Uzziah was king in Jerusalem over the southern tribe of Judah, and while Jeroboam II was the wicked king in Samaria over the northern ten tribes of Israel. Amos was by no means a social reformer — though he did preach against some of the social ills of his day, especially against excessive drinking and rich people oppressing the poor. Those were symptoms of a much more deadly disease: unbelief.

That's the problem God sent Amos to address. The book of Amos is loaded with threats of God's impending judgment against Israel and against all of the wicked, but it also reveals God's longsuffering, merciful, and forgiving heart, with such loving appeals as: *"Seek the LORD and live!"*[3] and: *"Seek good and not evil, so that you may live, and then it will be like this for you: The LORD, the God of Armies, will be with you."*[4]

Jeroboam II of Israel committed one particularly terrible sin. In order to prevent the northern ten tribes from taking their offerings of money and grain and their sacrificial animals down south to the LORD's temple in Jerusalem, he built two rival worship centers in his kingdom: one temple up at the far north of Israel at the border city of Dan, and the other temple way down south at the border city of Bethel, just a few miles north of Jerusalem. In each of those temples Jeroboam erected a golden calf, and he commanded the northern ten tribes of Israel to worship the golden calf at either Dan or Bethel. He

---

[3] Amos 5:4 and 6
[4] Amos 5:14

forbade the people of Israel to worship the LORD at Jerusalem ever again.

Both countries, Israel and Judah, were enjoying economic prosperity at the time, but immorality was rampant and the rich constantly oppressed the poor. God called Amos to leave his home at Tekoa in Judah, and he commanded Amos to go up north to Bethel in Israel and to preach against all this wickedness — especially against the idolatry which the Old Testament often calls *"the sin of Jeroboam."* The LORD was sending Amos on a mission of mercy to deliver this very serious message: Repent and return to the LORD for forgiveness and salvation — or else you will be destroyed!

Part 2: And What Do We Know about Amaziah?

Very little, actually. He was the priest at the king's sanctuary in Bethel where he served at the altar dedicated to the golden calf — a fertility cult very common in the ancient world, especially among Egyptians and Canaanites. Who appointed Amaziah to that priestly office? The king of Israel must have appointed him, for he ministered at the king's sanctuary. So to whom did Amaziah answer? To wicked, idolatrous King Jeroboam II.

Our text begins with Amaziah sending a written report to Jeroboam about Amos' activities, accusing of insurrection against the king and the nation. After all, Amos was preaching that the king would be killed in a foreign land and that the Ten Tribes of Israel would be defeated and carted off into captivity. That's a pretty serious message!

When Amaziah tells Amos to go back home to the land of Judah and preach to his own people rather than to the people of Israel, Amos refuses. He objects that he's operating on God's own orders, that God himself had called him to preach to the people of the north. It was God commanding them to repent of their wickedness. Amos protests that God himself had called him into this ministry, to warn his wayward people that, if they refuse to repent and return to the LORD God of their fathers, God will let the heathen Assyrians destroy their nation and take them captive, far, far away from the Promised Land.

Unfortunately, neither Amaziah nor Jeroboam nor the Israelites of the north repented of their wickedness. They ignored God's faithful servant Amos, and, as a result, God allowed the Assyrian army in 722 B.C. to destroy the northern kingdom of Israel and to remove the Ten Tribes from the Promised Land. God never permitted them to return. Centuries later God mercifully did allow some of their individual descendants to return and to live among the people of Judah, or to stick together as small family units not far from Judah, but the Ten Tribes as such were lost to history.

Notice the love and patience and mercy of God! Even when he knew that his Word would be rejected, he still sent his messenger to proclaim it. The unbelieving Jeroboam and Amaziah were without excuse. The lost Ten Tribes had no excuse, either. They sowed the wind and they reaped the whirlwind. They got what they deserved.

But Amos did not fail in his ministry! Here's a classic example of faithfulness being its own reward. Amos was a faithful prophet of the LORD, and the LORD was very pleased with Amos for being so faithful. Yet the LORD was not pleased with the unfaithfulness of the wicked.

Part 3: What Does All this Teach Us about God and about Our Relationship to Him?

First of all, God is gracious and merciful. He does not want to condemn anyone, though he may wind up having to do just that in order to remain both just and holy. Our gracious God much prefers to warn his straying sheep and to lead them back into his fold. God wants all people to be saved, but he twists no arms! God does not force anybody to fear, love, and trust in him above all things. God does not force anybody into heaven. God allows people to reject him and hate him and even to deny his very existence, if that's what they prefer to do. But God's greatest desire is that all people turn away from sin and Satan, and that they return to the God who created us all and who sent Jesus to save us.

Now God is very, very serious about his Word — all of it! — whether or not we are. He paid such a high price for our salvation, sacrificing his only-begotten Son on the cross to redeem the world from sin, death, and the power of the devil. Let nobody be surprised to learn that God's judgment is fierce and severe against everyone who tramples underfoot his precious gift of the Savior and who despises his generous gift of mercy and salvation through Jesus.

May that never be us! Let us always heed God's holy Word, repent of all our sins, give all glory to him and to his Son Jesus. Let us always receive God's Word with joy and bring forth fruits of faith and hope and love. Let us faithfully pass down God's holy Word to our children and to their children. For:

God Is Very Serious about His Word!

And may our gracious LORD always bless us with preachers who are as faithful and courageous as was the prophet Amos. AMEN.

The 9ᵗʰ Sunday after Pentecost

TEXT: Psalm 23

¹ *The* L*ORD* *is my shepherd.*
I lack nothing.
² *He causes me to lie down in green pastures.*
He leads me beside quiet waters.
³ *He restores my soul.*
He guides me in paths of righteousness for his name's sake.
⁴ *Even though I walk through the valley of the shadow of death,*
I will fear no evil, for you are with me.
Your rod and your staff, they comfort me.
⁵ *You set a table for me in the presence of my foes.*
You drench my head with oil.
My cup is overflowing.
⁶ *Surely goodness and mercy will pursue me all the days of my life,*
and I will live in the house of the L*ORD* *forever.* ✡

The Word of the L*ORD*. Thanks be to God!

In the name of our Good Shepherd, dear fellow sheep:

In the Eighteenth Century, during the French and Indian War, British troops became fond of mocking American colonists by calling them "Yankees." The song "Yankee Doodle" was written in order to make fun of our disorganized, disheveled colonial troops. A few years later during the American Revolution, General Washington's Continental Army was recapturing city after city from British control. Military bands with fife players would accompany the troops through the streets of each city playing "Yankee Doodle." That song quickly became our favorite American victory song.

We Christians have our own favorite victory song. It's in the Bible. It's Psalm 23, which clearly teaches that:

The LORD is Our Shepherd!

A thousand years before Christ, King David prophesied about the coming Redeemer, calling him our "LORD" and our "Shepherd." David was right on both counts! But:

Part 1: Who Is this "LORD" of Ours, Anyway?

Our English Bibles spell the words "Lord" and "LORD" in a couple of different ways. That's intended to let the reader know which Hebrew word is being translated in a given instance. This distinction is very important! "The Lord" spelled with lower case letters o-r-d is translating the Hebrew word *Adonai*. "The LORD" in all capital letters is translating the Hebrew word *Yahweh*.

- ☞ אֲדֹנָי (*Adonai*) means the Almighty God, the LORD and Creator and Ruler and Master of everyone and everything that exists.

- ☞ יהוה (*Yahweh*) is God's proper name. It is the four consonants *yod-heh-waw-heh*, which to us English speakers is an unpronounceable word since it has no vowels! Even the most scholarly rabbis have not known how to pronounce God's name for over 3,000 years. (Whenever the Jews see the word *Yahweh*, they always say *Adonai* in order to avoid violating the Second Commandment by misusing God's name *Yahweh*. They simply chose — and still choose — never to use it at all.) Even my pronunciation of *Yahweh* is just a guess. Other common guesses are *Yih-yeh*, or *Yehovah*, or *Jehovah* — but nobody except for God himself really knows for sure.

Yet what God's proper name <u>means</u> is quite clear. It indicates that he is the Law/Gospel God! He proclaimed his Law/Gospel name to Moses in:

<u>Exodus 34:5-7</u>: *⁵ The LORD came down in the cloud. He took his stand there with Moses and proclaimed the name of the LORD. ⁶ The LORD passed by in front of him and proclaimed: "The LORD, the LORD, the compassionate and gracious God, slow to anger, and overflowing with mercy and truth, ⁷ maintaining mercy for thousands, forgiving*

guilt and rebellion and sin. He will by no means clear the guilty. He calls their children and their children's children to account for the guilt of the fathers, even to the third and the fourth generation."

On the one hand, the LORD is very loving and merciful and gracious and forgiving. On the other hand, he is deadly serious about sin. He is the God of the Law which condemns and the eternally damns every sinner, but he is also the God of the Gospel of love and forgiveness and eternal life. His name proclaims that he is both! And this is the name of the LORD about whom King David is singing in Psalm 23.

Part 2: In What Sense Is the LORD Our "Shepherd," Anyway?

He tells us in our text, in <u>Verses 1-3</u>:

¹ The LORD is my shepherd.
I lack nothing.
² He causes me to lie down in green pastures.
He leads me beside quiet waters.
³ He restores my soul.
He guides me in paths of righteousness for his name's sake.

A good shepherd must provide sustenance for his sheep and lambs, and our LORD does exactly that. He provides for all of our physical and spiritual needs. Since he provides for us so well, we can say with confidence that we don't lack anything that we really need in this life because our Shepherd always provides.

A good shepherd must protect all of his sheep and lambs from the wolves and from all other predators and rustlers. They want nothing for us except death, destruction, and damnation. But the weapons which our Shepherd wields protect us from our old evil foe, from our enemies in this world, and from anyone and anything that might otherwise separate us from our Shepherd. King David sings in the fourth verse:

⁴ Even though I walk through the valley of the shadow of death,

> *I will fear no evil, for you are with me.*
> *Your rod and your staff, they comfort me.*

Our Good Shepherd will certainly also bless us with his grace in ways far beyond our wildest dreams. Even when surrounded by our enemies we can rest confident that our Shepherd is protecting us and providing for us. As David sings in the fifth verse:

> *⁵ You set a table for me in the presence of my foes.*
> *You drench my head with oil.*
> *My cup is overflowing.*

Yes, the cup into which our Shepherd pours his blessings for us is filled to overflowing. We are sipping from the saucer! We dine at the banquet which our LORD sets before us even when we are surrounded by Satan and all the wicked, because we're so confident that our Shepherd will protect us. And we know that we have a seat reserved for us at the wedding feast of the Lamb, and <u>that</u> feast will last forever!

King David teaches us to sing in the final verse:

> *⁶ Surely goodness and mercy will pursue me all the days of my life,*
> *and I will live in the house of the LORD forever.*

Wow! Such confidence we have — that we are going to spend eternity with our Good Shepherd in heaven; for Jesus, God's sacrificial Lamb, is at the same time our Shepherd.

Part 3: So Then the LORD <u>Is</u> Our Shepherd, Isn't He?!

- ☞ In times of want, he provides for us, even when we don't know where our next paycheck is coming from. And we can be confident of this, because, as the Psalm says: *"The LORD is my Shepherd. I lack nothing."*

- ☞ In times of plenty, our Shepherd moves us to return thanks to him and to share with those who are in need.

- ☞ In our youth, he leads us away from evil and towards ways that are God-pleasing, helping us to live according to the teachings of his Word; as the Psalm says: *"He guides me in paths of righteousness for his name's sake."*

- In our old age, our Shepherd comforts us with the Good News of sins forgiven and with certainty in what lies ahead for us: eternal life in paradise. As the Psalm says: *"I will live in the house of the LORD forever."*

- In times of helplessness, he encourages us and blesses us with healing and strength.

- In times of security, he reminds us that he is the One who makes us secure, now and forever.

- In times of sorrow, he comforts us with the good news of our own victory over sin, death, and hell — guaranteed by <u>his</u> resurrection.

- In times of joy, our Good Shepherd shares his love and grace with us, and he moves us to share that joy with others.

- And in heaven he will provide for our every need and fill us with joy forever!

A thousand years after King David wrote this beautiful psalm, Jesus came along and vindicated his words. He comforted his people, and still comforts <u>us</u>, with these words in:

<u>John 10:14-15,17-18</u>: *^{14} I am the Good Shepherd. I know my sheep and my sheep know me.... ^{15} I lay down my life for the sheep. ... ^{17} This is why the Father loves me, because I lay down my life so that I may take it up again. ... ^{18} I have the authority to lay it down, and I have the authority to take it up again. This is the commission I received from my Father.*

Yes, both in life and in death, Jesus is our LORD and our Good Shepherd!

Nearly every Christian would number the 23rd Psalm among his favorites. After all, that is our victory song, isn't it?

The LORD is Our Shepherd!

And we thank our dear Savior Jesus that he is! AMEN.

The 10th Sunday after Pentecost

TEXT: Mark 6:35-44

³⁵ It was already late in the day when his disciples came to him and said, "This is a deserted place and it is already very late. ³⁶ Send them away so they can go into the surrounding country and villages and buy themselves something to eat."

³⁷ But he answered them, "You give them something to eat."

They asked him, "Should we go and buy two hundred denarii worth of bread and give them something to eat?"

³⁸ He said to them, "How many loaves do you have? Go see."

When they found out, they said, "Five, and two fish."

³⁹ He directed everyone to sit down in groups on the green grass. ⁴⁰ They sat down in groups of hundreds and fifties. ⁴¹ Jesus took the five loaves and the two fish, looked up to heaven, and blessed the loaves and broke them. Then he kept giving pieces to his disciples to set in front of them. He also divided the two fish among them all. ⁴² They all ate and were satisfied. ⁴³ Then they picked up twelve basketfuls of broken pieces of bread and fish. ⁴⁴ There were five thousand men who ate the loaves. ✠

The Gospel of our Lord. Praise be to you, O Christ!

In the name of our almighty Savior, Jesus Christ, dear friends:

None of the four Gospel writers — neither Matthew, Mark, Luke, nor John — record every detail of the life of Christ. All four were inspired by the Holy Spirit to write their short biographies of Jesus to different groups of people at different times and for different purposes, so they each were inspired to select various events from the life of Christ that best suited their various purposes.

For example, Matthew and Luke are the only ones who even mention Jesus' birth. All four tell us about Jesus' baptism and about his innocent suffering and death to atone for the sins of the world, and about his victorious resurrection back to life from the dead, but only one other event in the life of Jesus is mentioned in all four Gospels: the Feeding of the Five Thousand. It is as if no account of the life of Jesus would be complete were it to omit this amazing event.

This miracle made a very powerful impression upon everyone who witnessed the miraculous multiplication of the loaves and the fish. Jesus used a great educational technique: He put a big problem in front of his disciples and he let them wrestle with it. They knew that the solutions which they offered were absurd, and they realized how helpless they were to solve the problem. When they concluded that they had no viable answer, they learned from their Master that:

Jesus Always Has the Best Answer!

The best answer:

Part 1: To Address the Needs of His People.

The setting was a big meadow on the southeast shore of the Sea of Galilee, sloping down from the Golan Heights to the water. Jesus had ridden in a boat with his twelve closest disciples across the Sea, trying to get away from the people, trying to get some quality time for teaching them the Good News of God's Kingdom. But the crowds followed him, walking — and some even running — around the eastern shore. They had witnessed many of Jesus' miracles — especially healing their sick and paralyzed and blind and deaf and mute. Some had even seen Jesus raise the dead boy at Nain back to life. They had heard Jesus' teaching and preaching, and they wanted to see and hear more. So Jesus continued teaching and preaching to the crowds.

When the sun sunk low in the sky, it was time for supper. Jesus saw their many needs, and his heart went out to the people. He did not chase them away; he gave them what they needed. When the sick and injured needed healing, Jesus healed them. And when these hungry people needed food, Jesus fed them. His disciples realized that the late hour was becoming a huge problem:

<u>Verses 35-36</u>: *³⁵ It was already late in the day when his disciples came to him and said, "This is a deserted place and it is already very late. ³⁶ Send them away so they can go into the surrounding country and villages and buy themselves something to eat."*

So Jesus set the problem before his disciples, and let them wrestle with it:

<u>Verse 37</u>: *He answered them, "<u>You</u> give them something to eat."*

His disciples did the math. They knew there were no cities nearby, and that the few villages in the area could not feed all those people. We're talking five thousand men — not counting the women and children! Sadly, this was the best that his disciples could figure:

<u>Verse 37</u>: *They asked him, "Should we go and buy two hundred* denarii *worth of bread and give them something to eat?"*

Jesus' disciples failed the test. They were in the presence of the almighty Lord, the Creator of the universe, the One who had all power in the heavens and on the earth. They had witnessed countless occasions when Jesus had answered peoples' needs and took care of their problems. And yet, rather than turning to Jesus and asking him for help with this big problem, they depended upon their own devices. They quickly concluded that they were helpless and that their situation was hopeless.

They were right! Two hundred *denarii* (silver coins representing 200 days' wages) would <u>not</u> have been enough to feed that crowd. Wise King Solomon had said: *"Trust in the LORD with all your heart, and do not rely on your own understanding."*[1] They should have trusted in their Lord rather than relying on their own weak human abilities to solve such a huge problem!

---

[1] Proverbs 3:5

The Pentecost Season

Yet in his grace, Jesus went on to fix the problem. He addressed the needs of the people and took care of them.

<u>Verses 38-44</u>: *³⁸ He said to them, "How many loaves do you have? Go see."*

When they found out, they said, "Five, and two fish."

³⁹ He directed everyone to sit down in groups on the green grass. ⁴⁰ They sat down in groups of hundreds and fifties. ⁴¹ Jesus took the five loaves and the two fish, looked up to heaven, and blessed the loaves and broke them. Then he kept giving pieces to his disciples to set in front of them. He also divided the two fish among them all. ⁴² They all ate and were satisfied. ⁴³ Then they picked up twelve basketfuls of broken pieces of bread and fish. ⁴⁴ There were five thousand men who ate the loaves.

Jesus addressed the needs of his people, and he had the right answer! He always does!

You and I have needs, too. Sometimes we despair of finding any good answers as we seek to address our needs. But Jesus <u>always</u> has the right answer! He <u>can</u> address our needs. He <u>does</u> address our needs! So why don't we pray to him and ask him to take care of our needs?

We need to pray, and we know that. We know that Jesus hears and answers the prayers of his people. Yet we often think that <u>we</u> have the answers to our problems and we ignore our Lord Jesus. When we <u>do</u> pray, so often our prayers are matters of <u>us</u> telling our Lord <u>what</u> we want him to do for us, and just <u>how</u> we want him to do it, and exactly <u>when</u> we want him to do it for us — as if God needed our advice! ***Jesus Always Has the Best Answer* to address the needs of his people,** and

Part 2: In Spite of the Weakness of His People.

Jesus exposed the weakness of his disciples' faith by setting this problem before them: Thousands of people had no way to make it back home without food. The disciples despaired of any good answer to their problem: too little money, too remote a location, and too few loaves and fish. So their Master Teacher taught them a very powerful lesson! When faced with this predicament, Jesus had the perfect answer, in spite of their weakness of the faith. **Jesus Always Has the Best Answer, in spite of the weakness of his people.** And his answer is always:

Part 3: In Keeping with His Abundant Grace.

Don't fret! Jesus has the answers to our problems as well, in spite of the weakness of our faith. In spite of our weakness and countless sins, Jesus does take care of our many needs. Though we are weak and undeserving, Jesus does shower us with his abundant grace! Just look at how he answered his disciples' dilemma:

Verse 43: *They picked up twelve basketfuls of broken pieces of bread and fish.*

Wow! That's far more than Jesus began with! Five loaves of bread and two small fish satisfied the hunger of many thousands of people, and Jesus finished with more food left over than he had when he began! What miraculous evidence of Jesus' abundant power and grace!

Most of those people were subsistence farmers and subsistence fishermen. In other words, they raised or caught barely enough to get by from one week to the next, one year to the next. We might say that they lived paycheck to paycheck. Where would their money come from? Though they thought that their biggest need was their daily bread, Jesus knew better. Our Savior knows that *"It is a terrifying thing to fall into the hands of the living God,"*[2] and that *"Man does not live by bread alone."*[3]

As imperfect human beings, we were all born into this broken world doomed for destruction, destined to spend eternity in hell with no hope of avoiding the eternal penalty for our sins. But Almighty God looked down from heaven and saw our miserable plight, and he had pity on us. His grace and mercy are truly abundant! In the words of the Apostle John:

---

[2] Hebrews 10:31

[3] Deuteronomy 8:3, paraphrased by Jesus in Matthew 4:4: *"Man shall not live by bread alone...."*

John 3:16-18: *¹⁶ God so loved the world that he gave his only-begotten Son, that whoever believes in him shall not perish, but have eternal life. ¹⁷ For God did not send his Son into the world to condemn the world, but to save the world through him. ¹⁸ The one who believes in him is not condemned.*

In spite of our weakness, our sinfulness, our thanklessness, and our utter inability to do anything to save ourselves, ***Jesus Always Has the Best Answer.*** **In keeping with his abundant grace**, he took on human flesh and blood to be our Substitute. He subjected himself to his own laws and kept them perfectly <u>for us</u>. Then he allowed himself to be tortured and executed to satisfy God's wrath against us and our sins. He earned eternal life in heaven <u>for us</u>! <u>That is grace</u>!

When his disciples could not solve their problem, Jesus provided his answer in keeping with his abundant grace. When we could not solve the problem of our own sinfulness, Jesus provided the answer in keeping with his abundant grace. Why? Because ***Jesus Always Has the Best Answer!*** He always addresses the needs of his people, **in spite of our weakness, and in keeping with his abundant grace** — his saving love.

So when you have problems, take them to the Lord in prayer. After all,

Jesus Always Has the Best Answer!

Sometimes, as a good father, he says "Yes," or "No," or "Later"; but you may be certain of one thing: Jesus' answer is always the best for us — whether we understand it or not.

In the name of our crucified, risen, and ascended Savior, Jesus Christ, who always hears and answer every prayer of his people. AMEN.

The 11th Sunday after Pentecost

TEXT: John 6:24-35

²⁴ When the crowd saw that neither Jesus nor his disciples were there, they got into the boats and went to Capernaum looking for Jesus. ²⁵ When they found him on the other side of the sea, they asked him, "Rabbi, when did you get here?"

²⁶ Jesus answered them, "Amen, Amen, I tell you: You are not looking for me because you saw the miraculous signs, but because you ate the loaves and were filled. ²⁷ Do not continue to work for the food that spoils, but for the food that endures to eternal life, which the Son of Man will give you. For on him God the Father has placed his seal of approval."

²⁸ So they said to him, "What should we do to carry out the works of God?"

²⁹ Jesus answered them, "This is the work of God: that you believe in the one he sent."

³⁰ Then they asked him, "So what miraculous sign are you going to do, that we may see it and believe you? What miraculous sign are you going to perform? ³¹ Our fathers ate the manna in the wilderness, just as it is written, 'He gave them bread from heaven to eat.'"[1]

³² Jesus said to them, "Amen, Amen, I tell you: Moses did not give you the bread from heaven, but my Father gives you the real bread from heaven. ³³ For the bread of God is the one who comes down from heaven and gives life to the world."

³⁴ "Sir," they said to him, "give us this bread all the time!"

---

[1] Psalm 78:24

The Pentecost Season

³⁵ "I am the Bread of Life," Jesus told them. "The one who comes to me will never be hungry, and the one who believes in me will never be thirsty." ✠

The Gospel of our Lord. Praise be to you, O Christ!

In the name of Jesus, the Son of Man and Son of God, dear friends:

If you've ever owned a dog, you know that they are insatiable! It seems that they are always wanting to eat. They like to worm their way between the feet of everyone at the dining room table, hoping for scraps of people-food to fall their way. If they're not sleeping or barking, they're jonesing for a treat, mooching a tidbit of anything edible. It seems that their appetite for food can never be satisfied.

Many people are like that, refusing to be satisfied. No matter what they get, they always demand more. Most people don't even know what they really need — what's most important for their lives in this world, much less in the world to come. Most people don't know how to prioritize their lives in a God-pleasing way. Most people are going through the motions of living without giving it much thought. But Jesus tells us in his "Bread of Life Discourse" here in John verse 29: *"This is the work of God: that you believe in the one he sent."*

Many well-intentioned Christians think that this section of God's Word is talking about the Lord's Supper, but that's not what's under discussion in this chapter. In fact, St. John never discusses Holy Communion in any of his five books in the New Testament. Here in John chapter 6 Jesus is speaking about the importance of <u>believing</u> in him, not about receiving the Sacrament. In this portion of John's Gospel we learn that:

Jesus is the Bread of Life!

This is very important for you to know and believe, because:

Part 1: Dining on Jesus Will Satisfy You.

Our Lord had just finished feeding five thousand men — plus their women and children — with five loaves of bread and two small fish. He underscored this tremendous miracle by providing twelve basketfuls of leftovers. The enormity of this miracle was not lost on the people. They recognized the power he was able to wield in order to feed their bodies. Just imagine if he were their king! He could provide for all their daily needs! What they wanted was a chicken in every pot, two cars in every garage, and a bass boat parked along the side of every house, so to speak. They wanted to take Jesus and make him their bread-king.

But Jesus was not impressed with their political aspirations. He refused to be the kind of king they wanted. He told them: "That's not the kind of king I came to be! You only want food for your stomachs, but I came to feed your souls!" He says it this way in:

<u>Verses 26-27</u>: ²⁶ *"Amen, Amen, I tell you: You are not looking for me because you saw the miraculous signs, but because you ate the loaves and were filled.* ²⁷ *Do not continue to work for the food that spoils, but for the food that endures to eternal life, which the Son of Man will give you. For on him God the Father has placed his seal of approval."*

It's true that God provides for our every bodily need. That's what Jesus says in the Fourth Petition of the Lord's Prayer, when he teaches us to pray: *"Give us this day our daily bread."* In his *Small Catechism*, Martin Luther explains what this means:

> God surely gives daily bread without our asking, even to all the wicked, but we pray in this petition that he would lead us to realize this and to receive our daily bread with thanksgiving.

When he fed the five thousand, Jesus gave food to everybody present, whether or not they believed in him as the Christ, the Son of the living God. The believers among them received the bread and fish with thanks, but the unbelievers did not. They merely continued their search for food to fill their bellies, and they saw in Jesus a man who could give them exactly that — but no more.

On the other hand, Jesus came to bless us with much more than food for our tummies. He came to bless us, as he says, with *"food that endures to eternal life."* The Jews clearly did not understand what Jesus was saying, and they demanded to know by what authority he said it. After all, Moses gave manna to their forefathers in the wilderness, right? What a miracle! What kind of miracle would Jesus do to prove that he had the same authority as Moses?

Jesus reminded them that it was <u>not</u> Moses who fed their forefathers in the wilderness with the bread from heaven. That manna was sent from God himself to provide them with daily sustenance. But that was then, and this is now. Jesus told them in:

<u>Verses 32-33</u>: *³² "My Father gives you the <u>real</u> bread from heaven. ³³ For the bread of God is the one who comes down from heaven and gives life to the world."*

So they said to him, "Give us this bread all the time!"

They wanted Jesus to fill their bellies and make their lives in this world much easier — but that's not the kind of Messiah Jesus came to be. He told them: *"<u>I</u> am the Bread of Life. ... The one who comes to me will never be hungry, and the one who believes in me will never be thirsty."* Yes, **Jesus *is* the Bread of Life,** and **dining on him will satisfy you.** What does this mean? It means that:

Part 2: Believing in Jesus Will Save You!

Now what does it mean to dine on him? Jesus answered this question for the Jews, and he answers it for us. He says that to dine on him is to eat *"the food that endures to eternal life, which the Son of Man will give you."* And how do you do that? By believing in him as God's Son and your Savior!

This is, after all, what God expects of us: that we should believe in his Son Jesus, whom he sent into this world to win eternal life for us. We do not — and we cannot! — earn our own salvation. God demands perfection, and nobody except for Jesus is perfect. In his Law God demands that we be holy, and nobody apart from Christ is holy. In that Law God tells us the consequences of our sins, saying: *"The soul who sins is the one who will die."* [2]

That's very bad news. I'm already a sinner, so even if I never sin for the rest of my life, it's already too late! I'm going to die and be forever separated from God in hell, because I am a poor, miserable sinner. And there's nothing I can do about it! Only a perfect person

---

[2] Ezekiel 18:20

can earn salvation, and I am far from perfect! Woe is me! I need somebody to save me! And the same is true for all of you, and for the whole world.

Praise God that there is a perfectly good answer to our dilemma! St. Paul says it this way: *"God was in Christ reconciling the world to himself, not counting their trespasses against them."* [3]   Jesus explains it this way to Nicodemus:

<u>John 3:16-17</u>:   *[16] God so loved the world that he gave his only-begotten Son, that whoever believes in him shall not perish, but have eternal life. [17] For God did not send his Son into the world to condemn the world, but to save the world through him.*

So <u>that's</u> what it means to dine on Jesus, the Bread of Life! It means to <u>believe</u> in him as God's Son and as your Savior from sin. It means to trust in the work Jesus did to earn salvation for you. It means to rely on Jesus' innocent suffering and death on the cross as full payment to atone for all your sins. It means to believe in the One who died for you and was raised again.

The Jews were always looking for something to <u>do</u> to please God, to prove that they were God's chosen people, to fulfill his Law just enough to qualify for eternal life. So they asked Jesus: *"What should we <u>do</u> to carry out the works of God?"* To which Jesus replied, *"This is the work of God: that you believe in the one he sent."* Are you looking for something to do to please God? Just believe in Jesus Christ, the Son of the living God. This will please God, and it will also please you! You see,

<u>Jesus</u> is the Bread of Life

and **dining on him will satisfy you.** Why? Because **believing in Jesus will save you!** AMEN.

---

[3] 2 Corinthians 5:19

The 12th Sunday after Pentecost

TEXT: 1 Kings 19:3-8

³ Elijah was afraid, and he ran for his life. He went to Beersheba, which belongs to Judah, and he left his servant there. ⁴ But he himself went a day's journey into the wilderness. There he sat down under a broom tree, where he prayed that he would die. He said, "I've had enough, LORD. Take my life, for I am no better than my fathers." ⁵ Then he lay down and went to sleep under the broom tree.

Suddenly an angel touched him and said, "Get up and eat."

⁶ Then he looked around, and near his head there was a loaf of bread baking on coals and a jar of water, so he ate and drank, and then he lay down again.

⁷ Then the angel of the LORD came back a second time and touched him and said, "Get up and eat, because the journey is too much for you."

⁸ So he got up and ate and drank. Then, with the strength gained from that food, he walked for forty days and forty nights to Horeb, the mountain of God. ✠

The Word of the LORD. Thanks be to God!

In Christ Jesus, the Friend of sinners, dear friends:

Have you ever been depressed? That's a silly question. Everyone gets depressed. Everyone feels miserable at times. There are times when it seems that everyone lets you down, or that nothing ever goes right. At times like these, arguing with family and so-called friends seems to never end. You experience problems with children or parents, coworkers or bosses, students or teachers, and you don't seem to meet anybody else's expectations — not even your own. You feel miserable and don't want to get out of bed to face another day. You might even think about going to the doctor's office or searching out a good counselor. God can seem to be very distant, and life itself can seem unbearable.

Well, my fellow Christians, cheer up!

God Makes Life Bearable!

So when life seems <u>un</u>bearable, pour out your heart to the Lord, and receive the strength that he offers you!

Part 1: Pour out Your Heart to the Lord!

Elijah was depressed. He had just defeated the 450 priests of Ba'al on Mt. Carmel in front of many witnesses. It was a glorious victory! He had every reason to believe that he had pretty much wiped out the biggest fertility cult in Israel. But when wicked Queen Jezebel learned about the slaughter of the priests of her own religion, she vowed not to eat, drink, or sleep until Elijah was dead, too.

When Elijah heard about the queen's wrath, he fled straight south into the desert wilderness. He sat down to rest under a broom tree. He was depressed. Apparently the fertility cult of Ba'al was not yet dead. When its champion Jezebel declared him an outlaw, Elijah <u>fled</u> rather than sticking around to defend the LORD's cause in Israel. He got no respect — in fact, he no longer respected himself. He had let himself down, and he felt that he had let the LORD down, too. Elijah figured that he was as good as dead.

So what did he do? He <u>prayed</u>. He poured out his heart to the LORD. He said in verse 4: *"I've had enough, LORD. Take my life, for I am no better than my fathers."*

And how did the LORD answer Elijah's prayer? First, God let his tired prophet fall asleep. That rest for his body and for his mind was a <u>tremendous</u> blessing. Then we read in:

<u>Verses 5-8</u>: *⁵Suddenly an angel touched him and said, "Get up and eat."*

⁶Then he looked around, and near his head there was a loaf of bread baking on coals and a jar of water, so he ate and drank, and then he lay down again.

> *⁷Then the angel of the LORD came back a second time and touched him and said, "Get up and eat, because the journey is too much for you."*
>
> *⁸ So he got up and ate and drank. Then, with the strength gained from that food, he walked for forty days and forty nights to Horeb, the mountain of God.* ✠

What do we learn from these words? When life seemed unbearable for Elijah, <u>God made life bearable</u> for him. This is what God does. <u>He makes life bearable</u> for his people, even when the problems we face in life seem <u>un</u>bearable.

Everyone has bouts with depression — to one degree or another. Some experience depression more often than others, and some feel depressed more deeply than normal. Psychologists and psychiatrists speak of <u>two</u> basic <u>kinds</u> of depression: <u>internal</u> and <u>external</u>. An <u>internal</u> depression is caused by a chemical imbalance in the brain — but this portion of God's Word is not talking about that. That's a matter for the medical professionals who specialize in that area, and that's <u>not</u> the kind of depression that plagued Elijah.

His depression was not internal but <u>external</u>. It was caused by issues and events outside of himself. External depressions often manifest themselves in feelings of inadequacy, failure, or worthlessness. The bottom line, it is often said, is low self-esteem. In other words, if you have an external depression, you really don't like yourself very much. You have high hopes, lofty ideals, and often unrealistic expectations of yourself — most of which others have taught you — but you can't deal with the reality of falling short of achieving those hopes and ideals and expectations. And since God's Word teaches that we all must live <u>perfect</u> lives, as Jesus did, your <u>guilt</u> pressures you into low self-esteem. You can see why so many mental health professionals have very little use for religion — especially for Christianity. They have some understanding of God's holy Law, but no understanding at all of God's holy Gospel! As a result, they totally misunderstand the Christian faith.

The Bible teaches that the root cause of our problems is <u>not</u> low self-esteem, but <u>our sinful nature</u>. God not only says that we must <u>be</u> perfect. He also tells us what he has done for us <u>because</u> we are <u>not</u> perfect. He promises his grace and blessing to everyone who trusts in his Son Jesus for forgiveness and salvation. God is so gracious and merciful that he sent his only-begotten Son into human flesh to live that perfectly holy life for us, in our place. Then he sacrificed his life on the cross in order to pay for our sins — again, in our place. Two days later Jesus rose back to life to prove that he's the Lord of life and of death, and that, because he lives, we shall live also. Death is <u>not</u> the end. Jesus proved it! We have much, much more to look forward to — not merely a six foot deep hole in the ground. Jesus won eternal life in heaven for us! Because of Jesus' saving work, our Heavenly Father has forgiven us all our sins and he looks upon us as his perfectly holy children. Again, <u>thanks be to Jesus</u>, our Savior and our Lord. He <u>already</u> took away our guilt, so guilt should never pressure <u>any</u> Christian into low self-esteem.

Christianity does <u>not</u> contribute to <u>any</u> psychological problems. In fact, it is the very <u>best</u> answer to <u>all</u> of our problems! Only the Christian, who knows that God has already taken away the guilt of our sins, can have <u>true</u> self-esteem. Jesus is *"the Way, the Truth, and the Life."*[1] Jesus is the only answer!

So when life seems unbearable, **pour out your heart to the LORD.** That's what Elijah did. And remember what God did? He strengthened Elijah for the long journey south to Mt. Horeb. It's wise to follow the prophet's example. The hymn writer Joseph Scriven put it this way:

> *Are we weak and heavy laden,*
> *Cumbered with a load of care?*
> *Precious Savior, still our refuge—*
> *Take it to the Lord in prayer.*
> *Do your friends despise, forsake you?*
> *Take it to the Lord in prayer.*
> *In his arms he'll take and shield you;*
> *You will find a solace there.*[2]

---

[1] John 14:6

[2] Joseph Medlicott Scriven (1819-1886), an Irish immigrant to Canada, wrote this hymn in 1855. It has been published in over 1,600 hymnals and translated into at least ten foreign languages. E.g., it's hymn #411 in *Christian Worship: A Lutheran Hymnal* (Milwaukee: Northwestern Publishing House, 1993). Public domain.

So **pour out your heart to the LORD!** Your precious Savior is still your refuge. Take it to the Lord in prayer! Tell him all your troubles, your worries, your heartaches. Yes, he already knows everything, and he already knows what you're going to say before you say it, but he wants to hear about those things directly from you! God is always there. He'll take and shield you in his arms. He's always ready to hear and answer your prayers.

But when you **pour out your heart to the LORD**, be ready to:

Part 2: Receive the Strength That He Offers You!

There's an old saying that goes: "When God lets us stumble, he does so that we may fall into his arms." Perhaps you know the truth of that saying from your own experience. Sometimes God lets us feel helpless so that we may be open to receiving his help. Sometimes God makes us face up to our own sinfulness so that we may more surely experience his unconditional forgiveness. And sometimes God makes us see how lost we really are so that we will turn to his Word for direction.

Now when God gives us strength, he rarely sends one of his angels to tap us on the shoulder and feed us. Instead, God strengthens our bodies with the food and drink that we need and the medications that our doctors prescribe for us. And God strengthens our souls through his holy Word and Sacraments.

Only in his Word do we learn about God's boundless love for all people — love which he proved by sacrificing his only-begotten Son Jesus to atone for the sins of mankind. Only in his Word do we learn of the many promises God has made to his people: promises such as:

- Nobody who believes and is baptized in the name of the Triune God will never perish. Instead, God will bless all of his faithful baptized people with eternal life.

- He promises forgiveness of all sins to everyone who trusts in his Son Jesus to come back from heaven in order to take us back to heaven with him.

- He promises to provide for our every need and to protect us from the devil and from all of our enemies until Christ returns to take us to his arms in heaven.

In the Sacrament of Holy <u>Baptism</u>, God made us his own dear children forever and forever. Through the washing with water and the Word, our sins are forgiven and we are made heirs of God's kingdom — and coheirs with Christ. Through this washing of rebirth and renewal by the Holy Spirit, we are marked by God as his chosen people and are rescued from the damnation that awaits this fallen creation.

In the Sacrament of Holy <u>Communion</u>, God feeds our souls with the body and blood of his Son Jesus. He gave his body into death for us. He poured out his lifeblood to cover all of our sins. Through this Holy Meal God forgives us our sins and cleanses us from all unrighteousness. Through this Sacred Supper God strengthens our faith in Jesus and in the many promises he has made to us.

The self-sacrificing love of Jesus is made most vivid to us in these two blessed Sacraments. These are the means by which God gives us his grace – grace to strengthen us, and grace to keep us close to him in the one true and saving faith. These are the means by which

God Makes Life Bearable!

So when you **pour out your heart to the Lord,** be prepared to **receive the strength that he offers you**. AMEN.

The 13ᵗʰ Sunday after Pentecost

TEXT: Proverbs 9:1-6

¹ Wisdom has built her house.
   She has carved out her seven pillars.
² She has prepared her meat.
   She has mixed her wine.
   She has already set her table.
³ She has sent out her servant girls.
   She calls from the highest point in the city,
⁴ "Whoever is naïve, let him turn in here."
   To someone who lacks sense she says,
⁵ "Come, eat my food,
   and drink the wine that I have mixed.
⁶ Abandon your naïve ways and live.
   Travel the road to understanding." ✡

The Word of the LORD. Thanks be to God!

In the name of Wisdom Incarnate, dear fellow invitees to Wisdom's banquet:

The Bible calls King Solomon the wisest man who ever lived, and the Holy Spirit inspired him to write most of what we call the Book of Proverbs. It's in that part of the Old Testament called Wisdom Literature. In Wisdom literature, Wisdom itself is personified — that is, Wisdom is given many <u>human</u> attributes, as if this abstract concept called "Wisdom" were a person. Wisdom is often contrasted with its opposite number, Folly, which is the devil and his wicked ways.

Now in many languages, including Latin, Spanish, German, French, Greek, and Hebrew, all nouns are assigned a particular gender — that is, every noun is either masculine, feminine, or, in many languages, none of the above — neuter. Nouns don't work like that in English, but if you have ever studied any of the languages I mentioned above you know exactly what I mean.

Why does this matter? Because the word which we translate as Wisdom is חכמה (*Khakhmah*) in the original Hebrew, and it is a feminine noun. So Wisdom is always referred to with the feminine pronouns she and her. Incidentally, the same is true in the Greek, where Wisdom is Σοφία (*Sophia*) — also a feminine noun. And yet Wisdom is a biblical name for Jesus! Every time "She" refers to "Wisdom," She is talking about Jesus. She is not calling Jesus a woman! It's simply that both Hebrew and Greek grammar consider the abstract concept Wisdom to be a feminine noun, so the pronouns which stand for Wisdom have to fall into line and agree with it in the same gender. The feminine pronouns are she, her, and hers. This is a basic rule of grammar. So Wisdom, then, is Jesus — as St. Paul says: *"Christ is the power of God and the Wisdom of God."*[1]

Today, based on what wise King Solomon says about Wisdom, I am encouraging you to:

Dine at Wisdom's Banquet!

But why should you? What has Wisdom ever done for us? Well, first of all:

Part 1: She Has Prepared a Banquet for Us.

Our text says in Verses 1 and 2:

> ¹ *Wisdom has built her house.*
> *She has carved out her seven pillars.*
> ² *She has prepared her meat.*
> *She has mixed her wine.*
> *She has already set her table.*

Everybody loves to eat at a banquet — especially when someone else picks up the check! And that's exactly what Wisdom has done for you. She's built the house where we will eat — a big, fancy house, since the roofs of most homes in Solomon's day (ten centuries before Christ) were supported by only three pillars. Bigger homes had five pillars, but only huge houses had seven. Wisdom has prepared the food and prepared the wine, and she has already set the table for you and for me.

---

[1] 1 Corinthians 1:24

Now <u>what</u> is this banquet Wisdom has prepared for us? Remember, Wisdom is a biblical name for God's Son, our Savior Jesus. He is, after all, true Wisdom incarnate. He is God's holy Word in human flesh and blood. In our Gospel reading today [2] we learn about Jesus teaching us to eat his flesh and drink his blood. In other words, we are to receive him internally, deep down inside, and we do that through faith in Jesus as our Savior. We are to read, mark, learn, and inwardly digest his holy Word; and as we do, we will be dining at Wisdom's banquet which our Lord Jesus has prepared for us.

That Wisdom is, of course, the Good News that *"God so loved the world that he gave his only-begotten Son, that whoever believes in him should not perish but have eternal life."* [3] We

Dine at Wisdom's Banquet

when we read or hear these words of the Gospel and believe these words with all our hearts!

Wisdom has not only prepared a banquet for us, but:

Part 2: She Has Also Invited Us.

<u>Verses 3-5</u>:

> [3] *She has sent out her servant girls.*
> *She calls from the highest point in the city,*
> [4] *"Whoever is naïve, let him turn in here."*
> *To someone who lacks sense she says,*
> [5] *"Come, eat my food,*
> *and drink the wine that I have mixed."*

With this beautiful imagery Wisdom invites us to the banquet she has prepared. Three centuries later the prophet Isaiah would use a similar metaphor: *"Hey, all of you who are thirsty, come to the water, even if you have no money! Come, buy and eat! Come, buy wine and milk without money and without cost."* [4] God always sends out his servants to invite his people to dine at his banquet.

---

[2] John 6:51-58
[3] John 3:16
[4] Isaiah 55:1

Jesus used this same illustration. In a parable about a wedding banquet he talks about how so <u>many</u> people come up with so <u>many</u> excuses for refusing to attend the banquet.[5] It breaks Jesus' heart that so <u>many</u> people refuse his gracious invitation to dine at the banquet he has prepared — a banquet which costs <u>us</u> nothing, but a banquet which cost <u>him</u> everything! That banquet is eternal rest in the kingdom of our Creator. When Jesus wept over the city of Jerusalem, he cried:

<u>Matthew 23:37</u>: *"Jerusalem, Jerusalem, who kills the prophets and stones those sent to her! How often I have wanted to gather your children together as a hen gathers her chicks under her wings, but you were not willing!"*

So very <u>many</u> people invent their own excuses to stay away from Wisdom's great banquet. Did you ever hear any of these?

- "I'm too busy to go to God's house or even read my Bible!"
- "I'm so busy earning my daily bread that I have no time left for the Bread of life!"
- "The preacher is boring!" or "The liturgy and hymns are boring or irrelevant!" Apparently Wisdom's banquet is not spicy enough or entertaining enough for some people.
- "Somebody else at that banquet hurt my feelings, so I'm never gonna eat there again!"
- "I already got confirmed, so I already know everything I need to know to qualify for heaven!"

Here's a newsflash: The quiz at the pearly gates will have only <u>one</u> question: "Do you repent of your sins and truly believe that Jesus Christ, God's Son, suffered and died to atone for your sins, that he rose again from the dead, and that he promised eternal life in heaven to all who believe and are baptized?"

If you <u>do</u> have <u>that</u> faith in your heart at the moment of your death, you will be ushered into the eternal wedding feast of the Lamb

---

[5] Luke 14:15-23

in heaven. If, on the other hand, you have lost that saving faith — if your Christian faith has been shipwrecked on the cares and pleasures and complaints of this world — then you forfeit your seat at the banquet and will spend eternity suffering for your own sins in hell. Is staying away from Wisdom's banquet really worth that risk? Jesus asked: *"What will it benefit a person if he gains the whole world, but forfeits his soul?"*[6]

Jesus wants to hold us close to himself at all times. He lovingly, yet urgently, invites us: *"Come to me all you who are weary and burdened, and I will give you rest."*[7] Remember: Jesus is Wisdom, and Wisdom has prepared her banquet. She has sent out her invitations, and:

Part 3: She Promises Eternal Salvation to All Who Dine There!

Wisdom says in verse 6:

> [6] *Abandon your naïve ways and live.*
> *Travel the road to understanding."*

Abandoning one's *naïve ways* means to stop living as we did before we were brought to faith in Christ — that is, before we came to dine at Wisdom's banquet. Or, if you are already a believer in Jesus, stop living as if you're an unbeliever! Dining at Wisdom's banquet gives us true understanding, and that understanding results in us turning away from our sins and living God-pleasing lives. Wisdom always leads us down the road to understanding, and the result is that we will live forever with our Creator and Savior Jesus.

Psalm 111 teaches that *"The fear of the LORD is the beginning of wisdom. All who do his precepts have good understanding."*[8] The *"fear of the LORD"* is faith in Jesus — in his suffering, in his death, and in his resurrection — all on our behalf. Jesus looked down from heaven and saw our greatest need: that we were wallowing in folly with no hope for the future but to spend eternity in hell. And in his amazing grace, he did something about it! God's true Wisdom from

---

[6] Matthew 16:26

[7] Matthew 11:28

[8] Psalm 111:10

all eternity took on human flesh and blood in the virgin's womb and became a man. He lived for us as our Substitute. He died for us as our Substitute. His suffering and death paid for all of our sins. On the third day he rose back to life to declare his victory over sin, death, and the power of the devil. Before he ascended back into heaven to prepare a place for us, he promised to return someday to take us to himself in paradise. <u>This</u> is the true Wisdom from heaven!

Jesus, who is God's true Wisdom in human flesh, has prepared for us a banquet of Wisdom in his holy Word and Sacraments. He has invited you and me and all people to his banquet. He promises eternal satisfaction to all who dine with him. Shall we not accept his invitation? Let us dine on this heavenly Wisdom! Let us invite our family and friends to join us at the banquet of Wisdom! Come, for all things are now ready! Come,

Dine at Wisdom's Banquet,

and find eternal satisfaction and rest. AMEN.

The 14th Sunday after Pentecost

TEXT: John 6:60-69

⁶⁰When they heard it, many of his disciples said, "This is a hard teaching! Who can listen to it?"

⁶¹But Jesus, knowing in himself that his disciples were grumbling about this, asked them, "Does this cause you to stumble in your faith? ⁶²What if you would see the Son of Man ascending to where he was before? ⁶³The Spirit is the one who gives life. The flesh does not help at all. The words that I have spoken to you are spirit and they are life. ⁶⁴But there are some of you who do not believe." For Jesus knew from the beginning those who would not believe and the one who would betray him. ⁶⁵He said, "This is why I told you that no one can come to me unless it is given to him by my Father."

⁶⁶After this, many of his disciples turned back and were not walking with him anymore. ⁶⁷So Jesus asked the Twelve, "You do not want to leave too, do you?"

⁶⁸Simon Peter answered him, "Lord, to whom will we go? You have the words of eternal life. ⁶⁹We have come to believe and know that you are the Holy One of God." ✠

The Gospel of our Lord. Praise be to you, O Christ!

In Christ Jesus, who is the Bread of Life, dear Friends:

During the summer of 2006, I studied in Quito, Ecuador, where the vast majority of people are Roman Catholics — but in name only. They almost never attend church — most of them only five or six times during their lives. But they still claim to be faithful Catholics, as long as "they made their first Communion," as they say. It doesn't seem to bother them whether they ever went to church in order to receive their second, third, or fourth Communion — as long as they made their first one. Local superstition is just as important to their personal religious thinking as their Catholic Christianity.

Several Quiteños [1] told me that they know and believe that St. Mary is far more important than Jesus simply because she is his mother and he is just her son. To prove this testimony of Marian faith, they point to the huge statues of the Blesséd Virgin atop the hills or mountains overlooking many of their cities and villages — for example, Quito and Baños. A huge statue of Mary protects each of those cities, you know; that's what the locals believe and that's what they tell you. They claim that that's the reason neither of those cities has ever been destroyed by the volcanos which cover most of Ecuador.

Mt. Pichincha, the big volcano on whose eastern slope the city of Quito is built, erupted in 1999. All the lava spilled over down the other three sides of the volcano, but the citizens of Quito were spared. The city was covered with several inches of volcanic ash — much easier to deal with than molten lava. Millions of Ecuadorians attribute that event to *"La Virgen del Panecillo,"* the huge statue of the virgin Mary which overlooks the city and which they credit with protecting it. (It's the largest aluminum statue in the world.)

About two weeks before I traveled to Ecuador in the summer of 2006, Mt. Tungurahua began to erupt. It continued to erupt every day for many months. That's just two hours south of Quito. A popular tourist city called Baños at the base of that volcano was spared destruction; all of Tungurahua's lava flowed down the other side. Apparently their huge statue of Mary has been protecting Baños, right? After all, three small villages on the other side of the volcano never had any big Mary statues, and those villages were quickly buried by mud slides and lava flows. Just like Mt. Vesuvius covering Pompeii, all of their inhabitants perished.

Ecuadorians often asked me in Spanish (of course) why I was studying Spanish down there. I always replied that I wanted to become better able to teach Spanish speaking people the Gospel of Jesus Christ in their own native language. They would usually tell me: "I don't know much about Jesus; I know much more about his mother!" Unfortunately, most of what they think they know about Jesus' mother is wrong. Even though they consider themselves to be faithful Catholics, they are in fact functionally non-Christian.

---

[1] Residents of Quito

Who is really the most important person in the world? Are <u>you</u> the most important person in <u>your</u> world? Is the President of the United States? The President of the Chinese Communist Party? Is the General Secretary of the U.N.? Is Mary, the mother of our Lord, the most important person in the world? God's Word teaches that <u>Jesus</u> is the most important person because:

Only Jesus Gives Eternal Life!

The words of today's sermon text were spoken by Jesus the very next day after his most famous miracle, the Feeding of the Five Thousand with only five loaves of bread and two small fish. The people wanted to take Jesus by force and make him their king. They figured that Jesus could provide for all of their physical needs.

"But that's <u>not</u> the kind of Messiah I came to be!" Jesus objected. So he withdrew to Capernaum, his adopted home town. "I did not come to <u>bring</u> you bread," he told them. "I AM the Bread from Heaven! Whoever eats <u>me</u> — that is, whoever eats my flesh and drinks my blood — has <u>eternal</u> life. If you do not eat my flesh and drink my blood, you cannot have eternal life!"[2] You see,

Part 1: Jesus Is the Bread of Life!

Bread has been the main staple food of life in almost every culture throughout world history. Since the dawn of time, one of the primary jobs of most men has been to bring home grain for the women to grind into flour. Since the dawn of time, one of the primary jobs of most women has been to take that grain and turn it into bread.

Then along comes Jesus, who says that <u>he</u> is the Bread of Life! Everyone who eats the bread — bread which begins as grain, gets ground into flour and made into dough, and then cooked into loaves — eventually dies anyway. But everyone who eats the Bread of Life — that is, receives Jesus internally through faith — will live forever. That is Jesus' promise!

You would think that <u>everyone</u> would respond: "Where can I get some of that bread? Please let me eat that bread!" After all, Jesus promises eternal life to all who dine on him — to all who trust in him

---

[2] Matthew 14:13-21; Mark 6:30-44; Luke 9:10-17; John 6:1-15,25-58

for forgiveness of sins and eternal life. But you see, Jesus _is_ the Bread of Life! Sadly:

Part 2: This Bread Offends Many People.

It offended Jesus' neighbors and many, many of his friends when he refused to be their bread-king, when he refused to be the kind of Messiah they wanted and which they thought they needed — a Messiah who would deliver them from the Romans and who would guarantee plenty of food in their bellies at all times. Jesus came to save his people — not from the Romans, and not from hunger, but from the eternal consequences of their sins.

That necessitates proclaiming the bad news of God's holy Law. You and I are sinners, and God hates sin. In fact, God demands blood payment for every sin we have ever committed, yet _we_ cannot pay God enough for our sins! No matter what we do, we are not able to satisfy God's anger. That's very bad news, and it offends the ears and sensitivities of arrogant, self-satisfied people. We are not good enough for God! God says that we must be perfect, that we must be as holy as he is, and no sinner measures up. We don't qualify for heaven, and there's _nothing_ that we can do about it! And there's nothing we can do to change our situation.

But praise God that _he_ did something about our predicament! God earned our salvation for us. He gave his Son Jesus, who paid the penalty which we could not pay. Jesus poured out his life blood on the cross for us. The fact is that _we_ belonged on that cross, but Jesus went there and sacrificed himself for us, in our place, as our Substitute. He paid our debt which we could never pay. He poured out his lifeblood to atone for all of our sins.

And now, thanks to Jesus, we are no longer offended by his cross. We recognize our own unworthiness. We turn away from our sins and leave them all at the foot of Jesus' cross to be covered by his holy, precious blood. We trust in Jesus' saving work to earn eternal life for us — a job we could never have done on our own. _That's_ the kind of Messiah that Jesus came to be! _That_ is the Good News of the Gospel. _That_ is the only message which saves us eternally. And that makes Jesus pretty important, doesn't it?!!

Part 3: Yet this Bread Is the Only Food Which Gives Eternal Life!

Verses 67-69: *⁶⁷ Jesus asked the Twelve, "You do not want to leave too, do you?"*

⁶⁸ Simon Peter answered him, "Lord, to whom will we go? You have the words of eternal life! ⁶⁹ We have come to believe and know that you are the Holy One of God."

Simon Peter had it right. The Holy Spirit had worked saving faith in the heart of this simple Jewish fisherman. Upon hearing Jesus' words and observing his many miracles, Peter had become convinced that Jesus really was and is *"the Christ, the Son of the living God."* [3] He knew that Jesus was and is God's Holy One. When so many others were offended by Jesus' claim to be the Bread of Life, Peter believed Jesus' testimony. By faith in Jesus, Peter ate the Bread of Life. When most others turned away from Jesus and rejected him as Messiah, Peter knew that only Jesus gives eternal life.

Eight chapters later Jesus proclaimed: *"I am the way, the truth, and the life; no one comes to the Father except through me!"*[4] Simon Peter believed those words! Soon after Jesus paid for the sins of the world by his suffering and death, and soon after his resurrection back to life and his ascension into heaven, Jesus sent the Holy Spirit to his Church on Pentecost. Shortly thereafter St. Peter testified to his Christian faith in front of the entire Jewish Sanhedrin. He proclaimed: *"There is salvation in no one else, for there is no other name under heaven given to people by which we must be saved."*[5] Peter proclaimed that Jesus, who is **the Bread of Life, is the Only Food Which Gives Eternal Life!**

So then, <u>who</u> is the most important person in the world? Jesus' virginal mother Mary was truly blessed because God chose her to be the mother of his one and only Son. For that reason we cannot deny her importance in the history of our salvation. Yet Mary is <u>not</u> the Bread of Life. <u>Jesus is!</u> Jesus is the only begotten Son of God, so by his very nature he is true God because he comes from true God. He

---

[3] Matthew 16:16

[4] John 14:6

[5] Acts 4:12

is God from God just as light comes from light. He is the One who worked out our salvation for us. He sacrificed his life for us on the cross. He defeated death for us by rising back to life from the dead.

That makes <u>Jesus</u> the most important person in the world. After all, he created us, protects us, feeds us, and delivers us from this sin-filled world. He is the One who gives us eternal life in heaven. Let us always rejoice to dine on Jesus — to receive him, the Bread of life, through faith alone. And through faith alone we will continue to receive all of his blessings — including forgiveness of all our sins, and eternal life in paradise! AMEN.

The 15th Sunday after Pentecost

TEXT: Ephesians 6:10-20

¹⁰Finally, be strong in the Lord and in his mighty power. ¹¹ Put on the full armor of God, so that you can stand against the schemes of the Devil. ¹² For our struggle is not against flesh and blood, but against the rulers, against the authorities, against the world rulers of this darkness, against the spiritual forces of evil in the heavenly places. ¹³ For this reason, take up the full armor of God, so that you will be able to take a stand on the evil day and, after you have done everything, to stand. ¹⁴ Stand, then, with the belt of truth buckled around your waist, with the breastplate of righteousness fastened in place, ¹⁵ and with the readiness that comes from the gospel of peace tied to your feet like sandals. ¹⁶ At all times hold up the shield of faith, with which you will be able to extinguish all the flaming arrows of the Evil One. ¹⁷ Also take the helmet of salvation and the sword of the Spirit, which is the word of God.

¹⁸At every opportunity, pray in the Spirit with every kind of prayer and petition. Stay alert for the same reason, always persevering in your intercession for all the saints. ¹⁹ Pray for me also, that when I open my mouth a message will be given to me that boldly reveals the mystery of the gospel, ²⁰ for which I am an ambassador in chains. Pray that I may speak about it boldly, as it is necessary for me to speak. ✠

The Word of the Lord. Thanks be to God!

In the name of Jesus, dear fellow soldiers in God's army:

The Spanish–American War was very brief, lasting only from April through August, 1898. America's war cry was "Remember the Maine!" A commodore named George Dewey led the U. S. Navy to a glorious victory over the Spanish in the Battle of Manila Bay. Future President Theodore Roosevelt and his Rough Riders famously charged up Cuba's San Juan Hill. In only four months Spain surrendered and the United States got Puerto Rico, Guam, and the Philippines. Spain was three hundred years past her prime when she lost to the U. S. in less than half a year. A major European power proved to be a pushover, and victory made the U. S. a major player on the world stage.

But we, the people of God, are in another war — a war which many people don't realize we are fighting because our enemy is largely <u>unseen</u> — a war which is far more critical to win than any other war ever fought — a war in which the casualties are much worse. <u>This</u> time the enemy is no pushover. <u>No</u> ounce of energy, <u>no</u> weapon, and <u>no</u> defense will ever be enough; because,

In This War, We Need the Full Armor of God!

Do you know which war I'm talking about? No, not the war we lost in Afghanistan. No. We are at war with an unseen enemy far more dangerous than any terrorists or any other human enemy:

Part 1: We Are at War with Satan!

<u>Verses 10-12</u>: *¹⁰ Finally, be strong in the Lord and in his mighty power. ¹¹ Put on the full armor of God, so that you can stand against the schemes of the Devil. ¹² For our struggle is not against flesh and blood, but against the rulers, against the authorities, against the world rulers of this darkness, against the spiritual forces of evil in the heavenly places.*

We are fighting the most evil empire and the ruler of darkness himself. We are at war against Satan — and he likes the way this war is going because his wily schemes are working very well! His enemies are <u>us</u>. <u>We Christians</u> are his enemies. Satan has plenty of allies in this world, and he has fooled many of us Christians into believing that they are not enemies but merely neutrals. The Devil has tricked them into forgetting what this war is really all about. But St. Paul reminds us of what this war is about. It's about *standing against the schemes of the Devil* and against his *spiritual forces of evil!*

Satan has confused countless human souls. The worship of Satan is a real religion in America. Satanic priests perform human sacrifices here in America and around the world. Time and again, police investigations attribute violent crimes to Satanic cult worship. The Satanic Bible is a best-seller on Amazon.com. Satanic music sells very well. Many young people buy it and listen to it without their parents knowing what it is. Most Satan worshipers in America today are atheists, humanists, and free-speech activists who use satanic imagery to oppose governments they feel are violating "separation of church and state."

Satan has tricked Christians into forgetting what this war is all about. It's about our precious souls and our eternal destiny! Satan uses the things and affairs and worries and pleasures and concerns of our everyday lives to divert our focus from the only One who can defeat him — and who has defeated him — Jesus, the son of Mary and son of God. Jesus is our only hope of victory!

We cannot defeat Satan on our own. Left to ourselves we would not stand a chance. He is far too powerful and smart for us. We cannot believe a word he says, for he has been a liar from the beginning. In fact, Jesus calls Satan *"the father of lying."* [1] Satan leads us into temptation every moment and leads us into sin every day. We need God himself to defend us! And, fortunately for us,

Part 2: God Provides Us with All the Armor We Need!

St. Paul reminds us in:

Verse 13: *For this reason, take up the full armor of God, so that you will be able to take a stand on the evil day and, after you have done everything, to stand.*

Paul teaches that we need to put on all of the armor God gives us as we go into battle against Satan. No half-hearted effort will do! Putting on only half of God's armor (like gathering around God's Word and Sacrament only once in a great while) will not do. Why do you suppose that God has given us so much armor? We all need all of the protection God gives!

Paul was very well acquainted with the armor of a Roman soldier. He lived with one during his imprisonment in Rome, from which he wrote this letter to the Christian church at Ephesus. Listen to the Apostle describe the armor God gives us to do battle against the Devil:

---

[1] John 8:44

Verse 14: *Stand, then, with the belt of truth buckled around your waist* (that is, the Word of God, which is truth). *Stand ... with the breastplate of righteousness fastened in place.*

The soldier's breastplate protected his heart. Even though <u>our</u> hearts are guilty of countless sins, Jesus gives us <u>his</u> righteousness as a breastplate to protect our hearts. He died to pay for all of our sins and, on that basis, God declared us righteous! When we believe God's Word and trust in Christ, <u>his</u> righteousness is <u>our</u> breastplate. Wear your God-given breastplate with confidence, because Christ's righteousness is yours!

In verse 15 Paul goes on to say that we should stand *with the readiness that comes from the <u>Gospel of peace</u> tied to [our] feet like sandals.* Roman soldiers wore sandals rather than boots — sandals that were tied firmly to their feet, ankles, and calves so they would not become loose or untied. The soldiers were always ready to travel at a moment's notice. Christians in Paul's day never knew when the next round of persecutions would begin, so he warns them to be ready at all times. Be ready to travel, taking the Gospel of peace between God and man to others — peace which Jesus established by his atoning sacrifice on Calvary. This same Good News will bring God's peace to many, many others, and it will prepare them also to do battle with Satan whenever he tempts <u>them</u> to sin and to give up on Christ.

Paul continues to encourage us in the next verse:

Verse 16: *At all times hold up the <u>shield of faith</u>, with which you will be able to extinguish all the flaming arrows of the Evil One.*

Before going into battle, Roman soldiers often soaked their leather shields in water. A soaking wet leather shield extinguished flaming arrows when they hit. With strong Christian faith shielding our souls, the devil's arrows will not burn us! In verse 17 St. Paul urges us to *"take the <u>helmet of salvation</u> and the <u>sword of the Spirit</u>, which is the Word of God."*

A wise soldier would <u>never</u> go into battle without wearing his helmet! Nor would he fail to carry his primary offensive weapon. Romans carried swords, and they used them to strike and kill their enemies. In our battles against the Devil, we must use God's holy Word just as Jesus did when <u>he</u> went to war against Satan. Jesus won the victory every time. Wield God's Word, and find comfort in your salvation!

St. Paul does not ignore the importance of prayer in our spiritual battles. He says in

<u>Verses 18-20</u>: *[18]At every opportunity, <u>pray</u> in the Spirit with every kind of prayer and petition. Stay alert for the same reason, always persevering in your intercession for all the saints. [19] <u>Pray</u> for me also, that when I open my mouth a message will be given to me that boldly reveals the mystery of the gospel, [20] for which I am an ambassador in chains. <u>Pray</u> that I may speak about it boldly, as it is necessary for me to speak.*

Paul says *"Pray.... Pray.... Pray...."* The hymn writer Joseph Scriven says it this way:

> Oh, what peace we often forfeit,
> Oh, what needless pain we bear
> All because we do <u>not</u> carry
> Everything to God in prayer![2]

Our war is not against flesh and blood. We are being attacked by the Devil himself and by all his wicked demons.

In This War We Need the Full Armor of God!

Why? Because we are at <u>war</u> — but not against human beings. We are at war with Satan! In this war we would not stand a chance, except that <u>God</u> is fighting <u>for us</u>. And never, ever fear! He provides us with all the armor and weapons we need. Our Lord Jesus Christ has defeated Satan for us, and he promises to share the final victory with us! AMEN.

---

[2] Joseph Medlicott Scriven, an Irish immigrant to Canada, wrote and published this hymn in 1855. It has been printed in over 1,600 hymnals and translated into at least ten foreign languages. E.g., it's hymn #411 in *Christian Worship: A Lutheran Hymnal* (Milwaukee: Northwestern Publishing House, 1993). Public domain.

The 16th Sunday after Pentecost

TEXT: Isaiah 35:4-7

⁴ *Say to those with fearful hearts,
  "Be strong, do not fear;
    your God will come,
  he will come with vengeance;
    with divine retribution he will come to save you."*

⁵ *Then will the eyes of the blind be opened
    and the ears of the deaf unstopped.*
⁶ *Then will the lame leap like a deer,
    and the mute tongue shout for joy.
  Water will gush forth in the wilderness
    and streams in the desert.*
⁷ *The burning sand will become a pool,
    the thirsty ground bubbling springs.
  In the haunts where jackals once lay,
    grass and reeds and papyrus will grow.* ✡

The Word of the LORD. Thanks be to God!

In Christ Jesus, dear Friends:

The year was 723 B.C. The Holy Land was inhabited by God's Old Testament people, the descendants of Abraham, Isaac, and Jacob — the so-called "Children of Israel" — but it was divided into two kingdoms: the Ten Tribes of Israel in the north, and the tribe of Judah in the south.

North of the Holy Land was the Assyrian Empire (pretty much modern day Iraq and Syria). Assyria was forcing Israel to pay them big, big dollars in tribute every year, or else. If Israel did not pay the tribute, the Assyrian army would wipe them out and forcibly march the people of Israel away from their land into captivity, scattered throughout their empire. When Israel's kings and princes formed an alliance with Egypt to their south and trusted the Egyptians to help defend them, Israel stopped paying that tribute. This infuriated the Assyrian king! He sent his army to destroy Samaria, Israel's capital city. The Assyrian army forced the vanquished Israelites to march hundreds of miles north and east, scattering them and resettling them all across their empire. Those came to be called the Lost Ten Tribes of Israel.

God allowed the Assyrians to do this in order to punish Israel for their wickedness, for rebelling against God, for their idolatry, and for trusting in the Egyptians rather than in the LORD. In their 250 year history, not one single king of Israel was a faithful child of God. Not one believed in the LORD who had rescued their forefathers from slavery in Egypt and had given them that Land flowing with milk and honey. So God gave them over to destruction.

Meanwhile, in the southern kingdom of Judah, the people saw what happened to their cousins up north. They were terrified that the same things would happen to them!

There was a faithful pastor in Jerusalem named Isaiah. God gave him this message to reassure the people of Judah that he would not turn his back on them, that he would defend and protect them, and that someday he would keep his promise to send his Messiah to them. God used Isaiah to teach his people how to recognize the Messiah when he would arrive on the scene. This is the charge God gave to his prophet, and these words are the text for today's sermon. Isaiah obeyed the LORD and passed along this comforting message to God's people:

Don't Be Afraid! The LORD Is Coming!

He will not only rescue you from the Assyrians:

Part 1: He Will Take Care of Your Souls — and Your Bodies, Too!

Once again, listen to Isaiah's comforting prophecy:

Verses 4–6^A: *"Be strong, do not fear;*
your God will come,
he will come with vengeance;
with divine retribution he will come to save you."

^{5} *Then will the eyes of the blind be opened*
and the ears of the deaf unstopped.

> ^{6} *Then will the lame leap like a deer,*
>   *and the mute tongue shout for joy.*

Through his prophet, God promised his people that he would save them, and he taught them how to recognize the Savior when he arrived.

Shortly before John the Baptist was executed by Herod Antipas, he sent his disciples to ask Jesus this question: *"Are you the Coming One or should we wait for someone else?"* [1] Jesus responded by reminding them of this passage and others like it in the scroll of the Prophet Isaiah. Jesus said:

<u>Matthew 11:4-5</u>: *^{4} Go, report to John what you hear and see: ^{5} The blind receive sight, the lame walk, those who have leprosy are cured, the deaf hear, the dead are raised, and the gospel is preached to the poor.*

Jesus referred them to our sermon text and to other passages written by Isaiah, who prophesied about the coming Messiah.

St. Mark tells us about Jesus healing a deaf mute. Mark reports that the people *"were amazed beyond measure and said, 'He [Jesus] has done everything well. He even makes the deaf hear and the mute speak!'"* [2] Every time Jesus performed miracles of healing, he was fulfilling Isaiah's prophecies. God does not forget his people! He sent Jesus to do the very things Isaiah foretold, and Jesus did everything very, very well.

Jesus is our Great Physician — both physically and spiritually. He not only takes care of our <u>bodies</u>, but he also takes care of our <u>souls</u>.

Part 2: In Fact, God Will Take Care of All Your Needs!

This is what God told Isaiah to say in:

<u>Verses 6^B–7</u>: *Waters will flow in the wilderness,*
   and streams in the wasteland.
   ^{7} The burning sand will become a pool,

---

[1] Matthew 11:3

[2] Mark 7:37

The Pentecost Season

and in the thirsty ground there will be springs of water.

When you stand atop of any mountain in southern Arizona, you look down on the desert floor around you. Most of what you see are shades of brown and gray, streaked with green vegetation in the low lying places. Greenery means that there's water near the surface. If there's <u>lots</u> of green, that means that water is <u>on</u> the surface — a pond or a stream, a lake, or a river, or a puddle that lasts a long time in the shade. Water is <u>very</u> important, especially in a desert. Water makes life possible. Nobody can survive, much less thrive, without a ready supply of water.

The land of Judah — the southern part of the Holy Land, with Jerusalem as its capital — is pretty much a barren desert; yet there <u>is</u> some greenery to be found. And wherever you <u>do</u> find green vegetation, you know that there's fresh water very near.

Jericho is called the City of Palms because of the many date palm trees surrounding its two big springs of water which bubble up year 'round. Those springs pretty much guarantee that somebody, someday, is going to build a city nearby! On the other hand, Jerusalem would not exist were it not for the many wells and cisterns and pools which men have dug or carved out of its limestone over the past three thousand years. That's what provides its citizens with water, without which Jerusalem could not exist.

But out in the Judean and Arabian deserts there are very few wells, very few pools of water, very few springs, and very few cisterns. There's very little rain and snow. There's not much water in that desert wilderness. That territory does not look like southern Arizona. It much more closely resembles the surface of the moon or Mars. It's pretty much a wasteland.

During the forty years when the Children of Israel wandered in the desert wilderness of Sinai and Midian, God constantly provided for their needs by giving them manna and quail to eat and plenty of water to drink. Yet Isaiah promises that when God delivers his people there will be waters flowing in the wilderness wasteland. There will be streams, pools, and springs. God will not only make life possible, but he will enable his people to survive and even thrive by blessing them abundantly, no matter how hopeless their circumstances may seem.

A few years after the Holy Spirit inspired Isaiah to write the words of this prophecy, the Assyrian army surrounded Jerusalem and besieged the city. They tried to starve out the people just as they had already done at Samaria. This tactic generally worked because Middle Eastern cities would run out of water and the people would prefer to surrender rather than die of thirst. But Judah's King Hezekiah was a faithful child of God. Under his leadership the Jews dug a tunnel to the well-hidden Gihon Spring just outside the city walls. Hewn out of solid limestone, that tunnel brought lots of water into Jerusalem's Pool of Siloam. This enabled the Jews to hold out for a long time. In answer to Hezekiah's prayers, God sent the Angel of Death through the Assyrian camp, and in one night, 185,000 soldiers died in their tents. General Sennacherib lifted the siege and took what little remained of his army back home to Assyria. God was faithful to his promises — just as God <u>always</u> defends and protects his faithful people!

God often provided water in some special, often miraculous, ways to "save" his Old Testament people. Here in Isaiah's prophecy God was promising to send his Son to save mankind. And as he always does, God kept his promises! St. Paul said it this way:

<u>Galatians 4:4-5</u>: *⁴When the set time had fully come, God sent his Son to be born of a woman, so that he would be born under the law, ⁵in order to redeem those under the law, so that we would be adopted as sons.*

That's <u>us</u>! In his mercy and grace, the one Holy God adopted <u>us</u> to be his children — now and forever. God the Father sent his only-begotten Son into the flesh through the womb of the virgin Mary to fulfil his holy Law for us. Jesus always loved his Heavenly father above all things. Jesus always loved his fellow human beings as much as he loved himself — even more so, for he laid down his life to atone for the sins of all people. Two days later, on that first Easter, Jesus rose back to life from the dead and declared his victory over sin, death, and the devil — and he did all for you, for me, and for all people. He brought the water of life to us who were dying of thirst in the desert wilderness of sin. He rescued us from eternal damnation to the burning sands in the wastelands of hell, and in their place he gives us to drink from the flowing spring of life in heaven. So:

Don't Be Afraid! The LORD Is Coming!

He <u>will</u> rescue you — your body <u>and</u> your soul. He will <u>always</u> take care of <u>all</u> your needs, just as he has promised. AMEN.

The 17th Sunday after Pentecost

TEXT: James 2:14-26

¹⁴ What good is it, my brothers, if someone says that he has faith but has no works? Such "faith" cannot save him, can it? ¹⁵ If a brother or sister needs clothes and lacks daily food ¹⁶ and one of you tells them, "Go in peace, keep warm, and eat well," but does not give them what their body needs, what good is it? ¹⁷ So also, such "faith," if it is alone and has no works, is dead. ¹⁸ But someone will say, "You have faith, and I have works." Show me your faith without works, and I will show you my faith by my works.

¹⁹ You believe that God is one. Good for you! Even the demons believe that — and shudder! ²⁰ But do you want proof, you mindless person, that such "faith" without works is dead? ²¹ Wasn't Abraham our father shown to be righteous by works when he offered Isaac his son on the altar? ²² You see that his faith was working together with his works, and by his works his faith was shown to be complete. ²³ And the Scripture was fulfilled that says, "Abraham believed God, and it was credited to him as righteousness."[1] He was also called God's friend.[2] ²⁴ You see that a person is shown to be righteous by works and not by faith alone.

²⁵ In the same way also, wasn't Rahab the prostitute shown to be righteous by works when she welcomed the spies and sent them out another way? ²⁶ For just as the body without breath is dead, so also faith without works is dead. ✠

The Word of the Lord. Thanks be to God!

---

[1] Genesis 15:6
[2] Isaiah 41:8

In the name of Jesus, the Friend of sinners, dear fellow friends of Jesus:

Martin Luther had a real problem with this letter written by St. James of Jerusalem, one of our Lord Jesus' half-brothers. The Catholic Church in Luther's day was teaching that sinners can only be saved from damnation and gain eternal life in heaven if they do enough good deeds — deeds good enough to please God and to cause him to overlook and forgive our many sins. They taught — and still teach — that Christian faith in our heart, <u>plus</u> many good deeds on our part, will result in our salvation. But Luther's primary concern was to return the Church's faith to the teaching of the apostles as spelled out in the Bible. The Bible clearly teaches that sinners are saved through faith alone in Jesus Christ, and not by doing good deeds. The basic, most important truth taught in the Bible is that God saves sinners <u>only</u> by his <u>grace</u>, and we receive God's saving grace <u>only</u> through <u>faith</u> in the Gospel of Jesus.

Luther studied this Epistle of James in great detail. He concluded that James focuses the reader's attention on our own good works rather than on salvation through the meritorious works of Jesus. For example, James says in verse 20: *"Faith without works is dead!"* Luther found this to be at odds with the chief article of Christianity: <u>justification through faith alone without any deeds of the Law</u>.

So Luther called this Book of James "an epistle of straw,"[3] but he did not advocate dropping the Book of James from the Bible. After all, it had been widely taught and believed by the ancient Fathers of the early Christian Church and it was still widely accepted. Rather than dropping James from the Bible, Luther suggested that it be dropped from the curriculum and not be taught in schools of theology anymore.

Luther's problem was that he did not understand St. James! But don't be to hard on Luther. After all, he was only human. Jesus was the only perfect man! Luther did not go to sleep one night as a Catholic and then wake up the next morning a consistently Lutheran

---

[3] *Luther's Works* 35, Word and Sacrament I (St. Louis: Concordia Publishing House, 1960), 358.

theologian. He continued to study the Bible throughout his life, and as he did, the Holy Spirit gradually led him to understand God's Word correctly — though Luther never fully arrived. Nobody understands everything in the Bible perfectly. We must continue to study God's Word as long as we live. Luther never really understood St. James. This book was something of a blind spot for him.

Luther also complained that James doesn't really teach about Jesus' suffering, death, and resurrection to save sinners. What Luther did notice was that James spends a lot of time dealing with the exact same topics that Jesus himself had taught. Jesus was big on teaching the importance of doing good deeds, as well as trusting in God for salvation. In his Sermon on the Mount Jesus teaches us to judge people by their deeds, saying in:

Matthew 7:17-20: *17 Every good tree produces good fruit, but a bad tree produces bad fruit. 18 A good tree cannot produce bad fruit, and a bad tree cannot produce good fruit. 19 Every tree that does not produce good fruit is cut down and thrown into the fire. 20 So then, by their fruit you will recognize them.*

Jesus taught that Christians must always remain connected to him in order to bear fruit — that is, to do any deeds that God considers to be good. He says in:

John 15:5 & 8: *5 I am the Vine; you are the branches. The one who remains in me and I in him is the one who bears much fruit, because without me you can do nothing. ... 8 My Father is glorified by this: that you continue to bear much fruit and prove to be my disciples.*

Jesus also taught about what will happen on Judgment Day. As the Judge of all people, he will not point towards our faith or lack of faith. After all, only God can read human hearts and see faith — or the lack thereof. Instead, in order to demonstrate the justice of his judgment, the Judge will point out the many good deeds done by his faithful believers, and the evil deeds done by all those who did not trust in Jesus for salvation. Jesus himself will be the Judge. On Judgment Day he will say: *"I was hungry and you fed me; I was thirsty and you gave me a drink. I was naked and you clothed me, I was sick and in prison and you visited me"* — *"or not!"* — etc. [4]

So since we are saved only through faith in Jesus, <u>why</u> will Jesus point out good works — or the lack thereof — as the basis for his final judgment? Because, as James says in our text:

Faith Without Works is Dead!

As I said before, the most important teaching of the Bible, the <u>chief article</u> of our Christian faith, is this: God justifies sinners by his <u>grace alone</u>, through <u>faith alone</u> in the saving work of Jesus, apart from any good works done by us.

So then, <u>why</u> would a just and holy God <u>justify</u> us sinners? Why would he declare us sinners to be just and holy? After all, we are in fact <u>sinners</u>!

St. Paul explains all this in his letter to the Romans: *"God shows his own love for us in this: While we were still sinners, Christ died for us."*[5] Sinners though we are, God has justified us — that is, for the sake of his Son Jesus, he has declared us "Not guilty!" of sin.

But <u>why</u> would the righteous and just and holy God do such a thing? What is God's reason for justifying us sinners? The answer is found in one word: GRACE. Only grace. God has declared us sinners to be righteous and holy simply because he is a gracious God. Grace is one of God's amazing attributes. It's one of his defining characteristics. Grace is the saving love of God for sinners. We don't deserve God's love, but he loves us anyway — and he proved it by sacrificing his only-begotten Son Jesus to atone for our countless sins. That's grace. We are not able to pay for our own sins, so Jesus came and paid the price for us. That's grace.

Now since he is true God from all eternity, Jesus owns everything. Yet, for our sakes, he set everything aside and became extremely poor. He humbled himself and willingly obeyed his Heavenly Father, suffering and dying on the cross to earn forgiveness and to win eternal life for us sinners.

---

[4] Paraphrasing Matthew 25:35-36
[5] Romans 5:8

Sometimes Christians use the five letters of the word "grace" as an acronym to explain what the word "grace" really means:

GRACE = G - R - A - C - E = **G**od's **R**iches **A**t **C**hrist's **E**xpense

Because of God's grace, everyone who trusts in the saving work of Jesus will receive all the riches of eternity in paradise, rather than being punished forever in hell. St. Paul explains <u>why</u> God did this for us. He says in:

<u>Ephesians 2:8-10</u>: *⁸ It is by grace you have been saved, through faith — and this is not from yourselves, it is the gift of God — ⁹ not by works, so that no one can boast. ¹⁰ For we are God's workmanship, created in Christ Jesus for good works, which God prepared in advance so that we would walk in them.*

So <u>this</u> is why a holy and righteous and just God justifies us sinners!

In his <u>grace</u> God created us specifically to do the good deeds which he has prepared in advance for us to do. St. Peter says it this way: *"So that you may proclaim the praises of him who called you out of darkness into his marvelous light."*[6]

To prove his point, St. James uses the example of Abraham. James poses this question:

<u>Verses 21-23</u>: ²¹ *Wasn't Abraham our father shown to be righteous by works when he offered Isaac his son on the altar?* ²² *You see that his faith was working together with his works, and by his works his faith was shown to be complete.* ²³ *And the Scripture was fulfilled that says, "Abraham believed God, and it was credited to him as righteousness."*[7]

You see, Abraham was a devout believer in God and in God's promises. He was willing to do anything for God — even willing to sacrifice his belovéd son Isaac when God demanded it. But praise God for calling a halt to that sacrifice! Thank God for providing a

---

[6] 1 Peter 2:9
[7] Quoting Genesis 15:6

ram as a substitute for Isaac! But the point that James drives home is that Abraham's deeds revealed his faith. The Holy Spirit had worked faith in Abraham's soul, and God credited that faith to him as righteousness. Abraham was justified only by God's <u>grace</u> which he received through <u>faith</u>, and as a <u>result</u> he showed his love for God by doing the good things that God required of him. His good deeds were his <u>response</u> to God's grace, <u>not the cause</u> of his salvation.

Then James brings up the example of the prostitute Rahab in:

<u>Verses 25-26</u>: *²⁵ In the same way also, wasn't Rahab the prostitute shown to be righteous by works when she welcomed the spies and sent them out another way? ²⁶ For just as the body without breath is dead, so also faith without works is dead.*

Rahab lived in the big walled city of Jericho when the Children of Israel were preparing to invade and conquer the land of Canaan. The people of Jericho had heard about the miraculous ways the LORD had been taking care of his people Israel: how he had led them out of Egypt through the Red Sea on dry land, how he had destroyed the mighty Egyptian army which was chasing them, and how he was providing for them in the desert of Midian. About two million Israelites were headed towards Canaan, and Jericho was in their way. When Joshua sent two spies into Jericho, Rahab cast her lot with them and with the Children of Israel. She had come to believe in the LORD God of Israel, so she protected and hid those spies when the men of Jericho came looking for them. James asks in:

<u>Verse 25</u>: *Wasn't Rahab the prostitute shown to be righteous by works when she welcomed the spies and sent them out another way?*

The clearly implied answer to his question is "Why, yes, she was! Rahab's works — her good deeds — <u>demonstrated</u> that she was a righteous person." Rahab <u>proved</u> herself to be a true believer and a child of the living God, just as you and I are. Her works — her deeds — <u>proved</u> the sincerity of her faith. St. James challenges his readers in:

<u>Verses 17-18</u>: *¹⁷ "Faith," if it is alone and has no works, is dead. But someone will say, "You have faith, and I have works."*

¹⁸ Show me your faith without works, and I will show you my faith <u>by</u> my works.

Only God can read a person's heart. Only God knows whether a person truly trusts in Jesus for forgiveness and salvation. But the works of the believer prove his faith! It's not that a person's good works are added to his faith in order to earn salvation. Good works do nothing to help anybody gain eternal life. They are the <u>result</u> of the fact that we are saved. God's faithful believers <u>do</u> good works! It's automatic! And, as with Abraham, God credits the believer's faith to him as the righteousness which God demands of all people, and as the righteousness God gives us through faith in Christ.

The only way to prove that you are really a Christian is by the things you say and do. God judges us trees by our fruits! And James concludes the whole matter by saying in verse 26: *"Just as the body without breath is dead, so also faith without works is dead."*

When you come upon the body of a person just lying on the side of the road, how do you know whether he's dead or alive? If he's breathing, that tells you he's still alive. If he's <u>not</u> breathing, that tells you that he's probably dead.

Faith Without Works Is Dead!

Faith which is alive <u>does</u> the good works God commands, the good deeds which God has prepared for us to do. Believers do good things for our fellow human beings, and we do good things for God, too. We do the good works God tells us to do as our way of thanking him for his blessings — especially to thank God for giving his Son Jesus to save us from hell and to take us to heaven.

What James is discussing — and what we've been talking about today — is called "sanctification." Sanctification begins with the Spirit's work of giving us saving faith in Jesus. After bringing us to faith, he continues motivating us to do the good works God demands.

Luther was <u>rightly</u> concerned about the Bible's teaching of "justification" because that's how God saves us sinners by declaring us "Not guilty!" for the sake of Jesus' sacrificial death to pay for the sins of the world. <u>Justification</u> is the chief article of the Christian faith because it <u>is</u> the Gospel itself. Yet most people in Luther's day had never heard about God justifying sinners, and, if they had, they completely misunderstood it because they were taught wrong.

But James is not talking about justification! He's talking about <u>sanctification</u> — that is, what the Holy Spirit does in the hearts and lives of believers. The Spirit sanctifies us. He sets us apart from the unbelieving world by the Gospel in God's Word and Sacraments. Everyone who believes the Gospel <u>does</u> the good deeds God demands. We love God, and we love our fellow man. It's automatic — just as Jesus said: *"If you love me, hold on to my commands."* [8] And what does God command? Love God most of all, and love your neighbor as yourself. [9] All of God's Law is summarized by, and included in, these two simple commands.

We are privileged to be heirs of the Lutheran Reformation, yet we most certainly <u>do</u> accept the Epistle of St. James. This is definitely part of God's inspired Word, and its message is very important for our Christian faith and life. In this portion of the Bible the Holy Spirit encourages us to live the kind of life which God has commanded. Don't just talk the talk. Walk the walk! After all,

Faith Without Works Is Dead!

In Jesus' holy name, AMEN.

---

[8] John 14:15
[9] Matthew 22:37-39; Mark 12:30-31; Luke 10:27

The 18th Sunday after Pentecost

TEXT: Mark 9:30-37

³⁰ They went on from there and passed through Galilee. He did not want anyone to know this, ³¹ because he was teaching his disciples. He told them, "The Son of Man is going to be betrayed into the hands of men, and they will kill him. But three days after he is killed, he will rise."

³² But they did not understand the statement and were afraid to ask him about it.

³³ They came to Capernaum. When he was in the house, he asked them, "What were you arguing about on the way?" ³⁴ But they remained silent, because on the way they had argued with one another about who was the greatest. ³⁵ Jesus sat down, called the Twelve, and said to them, "If anyone wants to be first, he will be the last of all and the servant of all." ³⁶ Then he took a little child and placed him in their midst. Taking the child in his arms, he said to them, ³⁷ "Whoever welcomes one of these little children in my name welcomes me. And whoever welcomes me, welcomes not just me but also him who sent me." ✠

The Gospel of our Lord. Praise be to you, O Christ!

In the name of the ultimate Servant-Leader, Jesus Christ, our Lord, dear friends:

Everybody wants to be Number One. Nobody tries to <u>avoid</u> winning the Super Bowl, or the World Series, or the Stanley Cup, or the gold medal. We were taught at an early age that "Nice guys finish last," so we do whatever we can to avoid last place — short of cheating, of course. Nothing awaits the guy who finishes in last place except for scorn, ridicule, and mock laughter. Knowing all of this motivates us to try harder, to dedicate ourselves to the task at hand,

and to give it all we've got as we try to succeed and win the prize, the trophy, the promotion, the championship, the prettiest girl, or whatever the prize may be.

Do you want to be a loser? Or would you rather be great? Of course we all want to be great! In our sermon text today Jesus teaches his disciples and he teaches us:

How You Can Be the Greatest Disciple

Our text today tells us about events which took place shortly after Jesus' transfiguration. On a mountain at the north end of the Holy Land, on the slopes of Mount Hermon, Jesus allowed Peter, James, and John to see him in all his divine glory.

Verses 30-31: *³⁰ They went on from there and passed through Galilee. He did not want anyone to know this, ³¹ because he was teaching his disciples.*

All this talk about "disciples"! What is a disciple? And:

Part 1: What Does it Mean to Be a Disciple of Jesus?

A disciple is a student who follows a master teacher, listening to his teachings and observing his way of life. He seeks to emulate that teacher's life style. At some point each disciple goes off and may himself become a teacher of others, gathering his own group of disciples. In this way the education process continues and multiplies, and the original master teacher's teachings and lifestyle are spread to many.

A great deal of education took place in the ancient world using this model. These were known as peripatetic schools, where master teachers led their disciples around and taught them. The world was their classroom. About five centuries before Christ, Socrates was a peripatetic teacher in Athens. His most famous disciple was Plato. Plato's most famous disciple was Aristotle. St. Paul, when he was still called Saul of Tarsus, was a disciple of the peripatetic teacher Gamaliel [1], one of the most famous teachers in the history of the Jewish people. John the Baptist and Jesus of Nazareth were both peripatetic teachers. Each had his own set of disciples, but neither of

---

[1] Paul talks about this in Acts 22:3.

them were trained at Jerusalem; nor were they authorized by the Jewish authorities to teach, preach, or baptize.

A disciple of Jesus is a person who listens to Jesus' teachings and believes his holy Word, just as it is written in the Bible. A disciple of Jesus is a person who regularly gathers with fellow disciples around Jesus' Word and Sacraments. A disciple of Jesus walks with him by emulating his lifestyle, putting Jesus' teachings into practice in daily life.

St. Mark tells us here in chapter 9 just how well Jesus' twelve closest disciples were doing at emulating his lifestyle:

Verses 31-34: *³¹ He [Jesus] told them, "The Son of Man is going to be betrayed into the hands of men, and they will kill him. But three days after he is killed, he will rise." ³² But they did not understand the statement and were afraid to ask him about it.*

³³ They came to Capernaum. When he was in the house, he asked them, "What were you arguing about on the way?" ³⁴ But they remained silent, because on the way they had argued with one another about who was the greatest.

His disciples did not understand Jesus' teaching about his single most important mission: to suffer, die, and rise back to life. Instead, there was rivalry among them about which of them would be the greatest in Christ's kingdom. Now, how does one measure greatness in Christ's kingdom? More importantly:

Part 2: How Does Jesus Measure Greatness among His Disciples?

He tells us in:

Verse 35: *Jesus sat down, called the Twelve, and said to them, "If anyone wants to be first, he will be the last of all and the servant of all."*

This is an example of <u>irony</u>. It's the <u>opposite</u> of what most people would expect. <u>Who's</u> number one? Jesus teaches his disciples, and he teaches <u>us</u>, that an attitude of <u>humble service</u> is the measure of greatness. He teaches this point most vividly with the following object lesson:

<u>Verses 36-37</u>: *³⁶ Then he took a little child and placed him in their midst. Taking the child in his arms, he said to them, ³⁷ "Whoever welcomes one of these little children in my name welcomes me. And whoever welcomes me, welcomes not just me but also him who sent me."*

That little child is a wonderful example of humility. He will do whatever the adult authority figure tells him to do, and he will do so willingly. <u>That's</u> the kind of humble service which God expects us to render to others. What a great object lesson for us! It's the same lesson Jesus had taught just five verses earlier, back in:

<u>Verse 31</u>: *He was teaching his disciples. He told them, "The Son of Man is going to be betrayed into the hands of men, and they will kill him. But three days after he is killed, he will rise."*

No follower of Jesus would ever deny that <u>he</u> was the greatest example of a humble servant. Yet for Jesus, greatness meant serving all mankind by willingly going to the cross; only later would he receive and accept the crown of glory. <u>First</u> he had to suffer and die to pay for the sins of the world, and <u>afterwards</u> he would rise from the dead and ascend to the Father's right hand. <u>First</u> the cross, <u>then</u> the crown. Just as Jesus says in the very next chapter: *"The Son of Man did not come to be served, but to serve, and to give his life as a ransom for many."* ²

President John F. Kennedy encouraged every American to aspire to greatness by committing themselves to public service and to sacrifice for the sake of others. His memorable words were: "Ask <u>not</u> what your <u>country</u> can do for <u>you</u> — ask what <u>you</u> can do for your <u>country</u>." ³ On a <u>much</u> higher plane Jesus gave his disciples that same principle two thousand years before! *"If anyone wants to be first, he will be the last of all and the servant of all"* (verse 35).

---

² Mark 10:45; also Matthew 20:28

³ In his Inaugural Address, Washington DC, January 20, 1961. John F. Kennedy Presidential Library and Museum, National Archives and Records Administration, http://www.JFKLibrary.org/Asset-Viewer/BqXIEM9F4024ntFl7SVAjA.aspx.

Sometimes we Christians — especially those of us who are very active in church work — seem to forget this lesson: that serving with <u>humility</u> is what makes us great in God's eyes. We work so hard and see so few others pitching in to help. It seems that most Christians just want to have a nice church building where they can go whenever they want to, so that they can pray, pay, and obey, but put little or no effort into the necessary day-to-day operations of the congregation. Sometimes we feel that we are getting dumped on or taken for granted by other church members who don't like the way we've been doing things around the church, or who have criticized, complained, or even pointed fingers when things aren't done their way. How would <u>God</u> have us feel? Should we <u>stop</u> being nice to them? Should we throw in the towel and stop serving others in the house of the Lord?

Just look at Jesus! Look at the perfect example of humble service Jesus gives. He came to serve by laying down his life for us, only to take it up again. He <u>lived</u> and <u>died</u> and <u>rose</u> again so that <u>we</u> might live forever. Never forget what Jesus teaches about the God-pleasing attitude of Christian humility: *"If anyone wants to be first, he will be the last of all and the servant of all"* (verse 35).

May God bless all of <u>us</u> with the humility to be great disciples of Jesus! AMEN.

The 19th Sunday after Pentecost

TEXT: Mark 9:38-50

³⁸ John said to him [Jesus], "Teacher, we saw someone driving out demons in your name. We tried to stop him, because he was not following us."

³⁹ But Jesus said, "Do not try to stop him, because no one who does a miracle in my name will be able soon afterward to speak evil about me. ⁴⁰ Whoever is not against us is for us. ⁴¹ Amen I tell you: Whoever gives you a cup of water to drink in my name, because you belong to Christ, will certainly not lose his reward.

⁴² "Whoever causes one of these little ones who believe in me to fall into sin, it would be better for him if he were thrown into the sea with a large millstone hung around his neck. ⁴³ If your hand causes you to fall into sin, cut it off. It is better for you to enter life maimed, than to have two hands and go into hell, into the unquenchable fire,

*⁴⁴ 'where their worm does not die,
   and the fire is not quenched.'* [1]

⁴⁵ "If your foot causes you to fall into sin, cut it off. It is better for you to enter life lame, than to have two feet and be thrown into hell, ⁴⁶ 'where their worm does not die, and the fire is not quenched.' ⁴⁷ If your eye causes you to fall into sin, pluck it out. It is better for you to enter the kingdom of God with one eye, than to have two eyes and be thrown into hell, ⁴⁸ 'where their worm does not die, and the fire is not quenched.' ⁴⁹ For everyone will be salted with fire. ⁵⁰ Salt is good. But if the salt loses its flavor, how will you make it salty again? Have salt in yourselves, and be at peace with one another." ✠

---

[1] Isaiah 66:24

The Gospel of our Lord. Praise be to you, O Christ!

In Christ Jesus, dear friends:

Very few people like to eat bland food. Almost everyone prefers food with some seasoning. Different people like different spices, and in a variety of combinations of spicy, sour, salty, sweet, and savory. Some spices are typical of a particular type of cuisine. For example: little red hot peppers are found in countless East Asian recipes; oregano, garlic, and basil are distinctly Italian; cilantro, jalapeños, and poblano peppers are obviously Mexican. Tabasco peppers are distinctive of Cajun food. Many Americans prefer to season their food with nothing more than salt, pepper, cinnamon, and sugar. I suppose that almost everyone prefers food that is seasoned with either sugar or salt, to a greater or lesser degree.

The Bible talks about salt in several places, and in every one of those places it speaks of salt's preservative qualities. Our sermon text today is no different in that respect. Jesus says in:

Verses 49-50:   *⁴⁹ "Everyone will be salted with fire. ⁵⁰ Salt is good. But if the salt loses its flavor, how will you make it salty again? Have salt in yourselves, and be at peace with one another."*

What about you and me as disciples of Jesus? Today we're going to talk about:

The Well-Seasoned Disciple of Jesus

Our Lord had recently taken his twelve closest disciples to the Golan heights and up the slopes of Mount Hermon. There they were privileged to witness his spectacular Transfiguration. After they left the mountains and returned to the Galilean plain, they witnessed Jesus exorcize an evil spirit from a boy. Then they started arguing among themselves about which of them was greatest in the kingdom of God, a topic about which the Lord had so often spoken. So Jesus taught them a lesson about Christian humility and humble service:

Verse 38:   *John said to [Jesus], "Teacher, we saw someone driving out demons in your name. We tried to stop him, because he was not following us."*

Jesus responded by teaching his disciples that

The Well-Seasoned Disciple of Jesus

Part 1: Encourages Those Who Are Weak in Their Faith and Understanding.

The Twelve failed to understand. They thought that they were the only ones who were allowed to wield the name of Jesus, to use Jesus' name in doing ministry, to glorify God in the name of Jesus. But they were wrong! Listen now as Jesus sets them straight:

Verses 39-40: *³⁹ Jesus said, "Do not try to stop him, because no one who does a miracle in my name will be able soon afterward to speak evil about me. ⁴⁰ Whoever is not against us is for us."*

Long ago I learned a good technique: Use absurdity to combat absurdity. When you combat absurdity by saying something equally absurd, it makes your point very clear. I've heard — and so have you, I'll bet — many people say things such as: "You people in your church think that you're the only ones!" Now what exactly does that mean? The only ones who will get to heaven? That's probably what they mean when they say something so absurd. I like to respond with something equally absurd: "No, we just get box seats!" That makes the point very clear. We certainly do not believe that we are "the only ones" going to heaven.

St. Paul says: *"If you confess with your mouth, 'Jesus is Lord,' and believe in your heart that God raised him from the dead, you will be saved."*² That's what all Christians believe. Everyone will be taken to heaven if he dies in this Christian faith! So we do not begrudge the growth of other Christian churches outside of our own fellowship; rather, we praise God that blood-bought souls are being saved and that Jesus' name is being glorified.

The Well-Seasoned Disciple of Jesus

encourages those who are weak in their faith and understanding! He also:

Part 2: Causes No One to Stumble — Especially a Child.

---

[2] Romans 10:9

Jesus continues in:

<u>Verses 41–42</u>: ⁴¹ *"Amen I tell you: Whoever gives you a cup of water to drink in my name, because you belong to Christ, will certainly not lose his reward.*

⁴² *"Whoever causes one of these little ones who believe in me to fall into sin, it would be better for him if he were thrown into the sea with a large millstone hung around his neck."*

Jesus reminds us how important it is for us to support the faith of the children in our midst. In Baptism God created faith in their little souls. In his Great Commission Jesus commands that we teach everyone who has been baptized everything that he commanded. [3] All of this serves to nurture the Christian faith of the Church's children. They're Jesus' own little lambs!

Our Savior warns us against offending the weak, especially the children who believe in him. Causing anyone — especially a child — to stumble in his walk with Jesus, to cause him to sin, or, even worse, to fall away from faith in Christ, is a terrible thing to do! Our Lord says, *"It would be better for him if he were thrown into the sea with a large millstone hung around his neck."* Millstones weigh hundreds of pounds. You get the picture. Don't do anything to prevent or even discourage Jesus' little lambs from coming to him and believing in him! Instead, God commands us to *"bring them up in the training and instruction of the Lord."*[4]

In the next several verses, Jesus talks about causing other people to sin by <u>our own</u> sins:

<u>Verses 43-48</u>: ⁴³ *"If your hand causes you to fall into sin, cut it off. It is better for you to enter life maimed, than to have two hands and go into hell, into the unquenchable fire,*

⁴⁴ *'where their worm does not die,
    and the fire is not quenched.'* [5]

---

[3] cf. Matthew 28:19-20

[4] Ephesians 6:4

[5] quoting Isaiah 66:24

⁴⁵ "If your foot causes you to fall into sin, cut it off. It is better for you to enter life lame, than to have two feet and be thrown into hell, ⁴⁶ 'where their worm does not die, and the fire is not quenched.' ⁴⁷ If your eye causes you to fall into sin, pluck it out. It is better for you to enter the kingdom of God with one eye, than to have two eyes and be thrown into hell, ⁴⁸ 'where their worm does not die, and the fire is not quenched.'"

What's he saying? Cut off your hand? Cut off your foot? Pluck out your eyeball? Jesus is clearly not opposed to using hyperbole. One might even say that he's using absurdity to combat something equally absurd. The very idea that your hand, your foot, or your eye might <u>cause</u> you to sin is absurd, right? Because, you see, the problem is never really your hand, nor your foot, nor your eye. It's always your sin-filled human heart. As Jesus says in:

<u>Matthew 15:19-20</u>: *¹⁹ "To be sure, out of the heart come evil thoughts, murders, adulteries, sexual sins, thefts, false testimonies, and blasphemies. ²⁰ These are the things that defile a person."*

The Well-Seasoned Disciple of Jesus

encourages those who are weak in their faith and in their understanding, and he causes no one to stumble — especially not children. That's because:

The Well-Seasoned Disciple

is also:

Part 3: Filled with God's Word.

Once again, what is it that makes us Christians different from the rest of the world? It's not our holy lives. Let's face it: We still sin. Sinning is what sinners do. That does not excuse it, but it does explain it. Praise God that we have the antidote! God gives us the antidote in his holy Word: *"If we confess our sins, he is faithful and just to forgive us our sins and to cleanse us from all unrighteousness."*[6]

When we have spiritual questions, God's holy Word is where we'll find the answers. When we need spiritual direction, God's Law is there to teach us which way we should go. When we need God's counsel and strength, the Gospel of Jesus is written there to bless us with forgiveness of our sins and comfort from the Holy Spirit.

St. John says that everything that Jesus said or did in the New Testament has been *"written that you may believe that Jesus is the Christ, the Son of God, and that by believing you may have life in his name."*[7] St. Paul tells us <u>why</u> it's so very important for us to be filled with God's Word. He says in:

2 Timothy 3:15-17: *[15] "The Holy Scriptures ... are able to make you wise for salvation through faith in Christ Jesus. [16] All Scripture is God breathed and is useful for teaching, for rebuking, for correcting, and for training in righteousness, [17] so that the man of God may be complete, well equipped for every good work."*

The Well-Seasoned Disciple of Jesus
is filled with God's Word!

Our Lord says in:

Verses 49-50: [49] *"Everyone will be salted with fire. [50] Salt is good. But if the salt loses its flavor, how will you make it salty again? Have salt in yourselves, and be at peace with one another."*

What makes Christians "salty" is that we have been blessed by the Spirit with God's Word — with his Law and Gospel. By his grace we know what God commands and forbids, and we know that we have been forgiven by Jesus for our many sins against his commandments. He has also commissioned us to take his Law and Gospel out into the world and to gather disciples from all nations around his Word and Sacraments.

---

[6] 1 John 1:9

[7] John 20:31

But what if we Christians lose our saltiness? What if we trade our mission of proclaiming God's Law and Gospel for trying our level best to establish "social justice" and "community"? If the Church's focus is to fix people's problems in this life while ignoring their real problem in the life to come, we will have lost our saltiness and we will have done mankind a huge disservice! If our efforts are all about correcting what is wrong with this broken society and fallen world, we will have neglected the Kingdom of God and we will never be salty again!

Jesus said that we are *salty*, and he warns us not to lose our *flavor.* So let us never lose our saltiness — the flavor that Jesus made us to be! He has seasoned us very, very well by calling us to be his disciples. Let us always be filled with God's Word, and let us share that salt with others. AMEN.

The 20ᵗʰ Sunday after Pentecost

TEXT: Mark 10:13-16

¹³ Some people began bringing little children to Jesus so that he would touch them. But the disciples rebuked them. ¹⁴ When Jesus saw this, he was indignant. He said, "Let the little children come to me! Do not hinder them, because the kingdom of God belongs to such as these. ¹⁵ Amen I tell you: Whoever will not receive the kingdom of God like a little child will never enter it." ¹⁶ And he took the little children in his arms, laid his hands on them, and blessed them. ✠

The Gospel of our Lord. Praise be to you, O Christ!

In Christ Jesus, dear children of the living God:

There is an old saying that "Children are to be seen and not heard." Sadly, these words reflect an attitude which is all too common in our society — that children are an annoying inconvenience and that no sane adult should waste his time talking with them. Our hectic life-styles foster such an attitude. It seems that there's always something going on: work, meetings, gardening, shopping, cleaning house, traffic hassles, bowling, softball, card games, vacations, visits with friends and relatives — none of these are bad in and of themselves. In fact, most are good and even necessary, though our lives go by at such a feverish pace that children often get the short end of the stick. In our hectic world it seems that we seldom have much time for kids. Yet in our text Jesus showed his disciples and he shows us that

Jesus Always Has Time for Kids!

1) He Invites Them to Come to Him; and
2) He Blesses Them When They Are Brought to Him.

Our text begins with Jesus teaching a crowd of people in a house in Judea. Word spread quickly that Jesus was in town. The Pharisees went to the house and tried to trick Jesus into saying something that they could use against him, but he quoted Scripture and sent them away. He went back into the house and continued teaching. People kept coming to the door wanting to see him, bringing their babies and small children. The people kept coming and coming. They knew that Jesus was inside that house, and they wanted him to bless their children. They expected him to lay his hands on them and bless them. That was really an act of faith on the part of the parents. They knew the blessings which Jesus had to offer, and they wanted their children to have those blessings, too.

But Jesus' disciples blocked the door, denying access to Jesus. They rebuked the parents. They must have said something like, "Are you crazy? Jesus is a busy man! He doesn't have time to waste on little kids who probably won't understand a word anyway! Take your kids home!" The disciples made the mistake of thinking that little children are insignificant and unimportant to the Lord. They made the mistake of thinking that Jesus has no time for kids.

When Jesus heard what was going on at the door, he was indignant. He was very displeased with his disciples for assuming that he was too busy to take time out for the children. He rebuked his disciples. He said in:

Verse 14:   Let the little children come to me! Do not hinder them, because the kingdom of God belongs to such as these.

Jesus made it perfectly clear to everyone that he always has time for kids!

Jesus used this opportunity to invite children of all ages to come to him, because children — including little babies — are definitely included in God's kingdom. To emphasize his invitation, he states it both positively — *"Let the little children come to me!"* and negatively — *"Do not hinder them."* So we see how important Jesus considers it that the children be brought to him. Those little lambs are precious to our Good Shepherd!

Jesus Always Has Time for Kids!

Do you have time for kids? Jesus does! He invites them to come to him. He wants nothing to hinder them, stop them, or in any way prevent them from coming to him. How important do you consider the children of our congregation? How important are your own children and grandchildren? God considers them very important — so important that he not only gave them to you as wonderful blessings, but he also took their sinful natures upon himself and suffered and died to pay for them, just as he paid for our sinful natures, too. Jesus gave his life as a ransom for babies as well as for adults, and for everyone in between. Jesus paid the exact same price for the souls of little children as he paid for the soul of every adult. Every single soul cost him his holy, precious blood, which he poured out for the whole world on Calvary's cross. Children are just as important to Jesus as anybody else!

It's easy for us to think that we're taking good care of our children when we give them food, clothing, and shelter, and when we lavish lots of worldly things upon them. But we are not doing the kind of parenting that God demands of us unless we also lavish "spiritual things" on them — that is, the Gospel in Word and Sacraments. If we don't give these "spiritual things" our priority, then we're telling our kids that God is not very important and he does not need to be the highest priority in their lives. And when they fall away from church right after confirmation (sometimes even before), whose fault is it? Have we taught our children to prioritize God's holy Word and Sacraments? Have we taught them to keep the Sabbath day holy — that is, set apart for God's holy Word?

Jesus wants us to bring our children to him so that they may receive the one thing needful — instruction in God's holy Word. This is the only way they can mature in their baptismal faith. This is the only way that they can learn about Jesus, the Son of God, the Savior of the world! Remember, without faith in Jesus, all people are doomed to eternal separation from the Creator.

Your attitude toward God's Word will be impressed upon your children's hearts. Set a God-pleasing example by showing them how you accept Jesus' invitation to meet with him at every opportunity, both at church and at home. Bring your children faithfully to Jesus by making use of our congregation's youth education programs and especially the divine services of God's house. Bring your infants to Jesus by having them baptized into God's family very, very soon after they are born. Teach your children to pray regularly and often.

THE PENTECOST SEASON

Model it for them! Make time in your busy life to read Bible stories to them, and take time to explain to them the simple truths of God's Word.

Do the same things for your grandchildren! Teach them to accept Jesus' invitation. God not only invites children to come to him, but he also blesses them when they do.

Right after Jesus emphatically invited the children, he continued by explaining more fully the nature of his kingdom. He said in:

Verses 14-15: *... the kingdom of God belongs to such as <u>these</u>. Amen I tell you: Whoever will not receive the kingdom of God like a little child will never enter it.*

He's saying that God's kingdom is made up of people *"such as these"* little children. Children are important to God! He not only includes them in his kingdom, but he also uses them as role models for <u>us</u> and for everyone who wants a part in God's kingdom. Jesus says that, if we want to get to heaven, we must receive God's kingdom in the same manner as a little child receives it — through simple, childlike faith, not doubting but firmly believing everything that Jesus teaches us in his Word.

Consider the faith of a child. How easily a little child believes in myths such as Santa Claus, the Easter Bunny, and the Tooth Fairy. Little children readily believe these myths without questioning simply because they trust what their parents tell them. The fact that nobody has ever seen reindeer fly makes no difference to the child. He's not bothered by such logic. This is the kind of faith which God demands of those who would enter his kingdom — not a faith built on evidence and reason, but a faith which is built on and which clings to our Heavenly Father's promises of forgiveness and eternal life, guaranteed by his son Jesus who died for us and was raised again — even though we have never seen a dead man raised back to life. Without this kind of <u>faith</u> — this childlike <u>trust</u> — Jesus tells us that we *"will never enter"* God's kingdom.

In the last verse of our text, St. Mark tells us that Jesus *"took the little children in his arms, laid his hands on them, and blessed them."* Our Savior loves kids. We can easily picture him picking up the children one by one, holding each of them in his arms, and putting his hand on each child's head. He pronounced his blessing upon each of them. We'll never know exactly what words Jesus used, but we can be sure that he gave each child a greater measure of the gifts of the Spirit — especially the gift of faith, so that they might grow in their conviction that Jesus is their Savior, and that Jesus gives them eternal life. Jesus fulfilled the expectations of the parents who brought their children to him. Even though he was very busy, Jesus <u>made</u> time to bless them!

Whenever we bring our children to Jesus, we can expect his blessing. He promised to bless everyone who believes and is baptized — including little children. He will bless them with <u>growth</u>: growth in faith, in knowledge, and in understanding of God's Word. He will bless them with <u>joy</u> in knowing that God loves us <u>all</u> and is very concerned about our welfare. He'll bless them with the privilege to talk to their Heavenly Father in <u>prayer</u>, confident that he will hear and answer. He will bless them with <u>courage</u> to witness their Christian faith to others. He'll bless them with a proper <u>understanding</u> of the sinful world in which we live and with a Christian <u>outlook</u> on life. He will bless them with the <u>fellowship</u> of Christian friends and parents, and hopefully also a Christian <u>spouse</u>. The list of his blessings goes on and on, and they are all of eternal value.

Unbelievers don't see much sense in trying to obtain these blessings for their children because their eyes are fixed only on the needs and pleasures of this world, but not on eternal matters. Yet Jesus asks: *"What will it benefit a person if he gains the whole world, but forfeits his soul?"*[1] We Christians know the grace and the blessings of our Savior Jesus, and we want those same blessings for our children — and for our grandchildren, too! So we maintain Christian schools and other youth ministries in order to procure the blessings of citizenship in God's kingdom for our children, and to lead other children to Jesus as well.

The <u>primary</u> purpose of Christian schools and youth ministries is to <u>assist</u> parents in fulfilling <u>their</u> God-given obligation to raise <u>their</u> children in the training and instruction of the Lord. Let's keep this in perspective. Christian education begins at home! We must

---

[1] Matthew 16:26

not abdicate our responsibility and leave our children's Christian education to the Church by default. Instead, let us focus our attention on the Christian upbringing of the children in our families and in our congregations. Let us be wise stewards of the blessings God has given us by making faithful use of our church's worship services, Christian schools, and youth ministries.

No matter how hectic life gets, we need to emulate our Savior.

Jesus Always Has Time for Kids!

So may we always have time for kids, too! AMEN.

The 21ˢᵗ Sunday after Pentecost

TEXT: Mark 10:17-27

¹⁷ As Jesus was setting out on a journey, one man ran up to him and knelt in front of him. He asked, "Good teacher, what must I do to inherit eternal life?"

¹⁸ Jesus said to him, "Why do you call me good? No one is good except one — God. ¹⁹ You know the commandments. 'You shall not murder. You shall not commit adultery. You shall not steal. You shall not give false testimony. You shall not defraud. Honor your father and mother.'"[1]

²⁰ The man replied, "Teacher, I have kept all these since I was a child."

²¹ Jesus looked at him, loved him, and said to him, "One thing you lack. Go, sell whatever you have, and give to the poor, and you will have treasure in heaven. Then come, follow me."

²² When he heard this, he looked sad and went away grieving, because he had great wealth. ²³ Jesus looked around and said to his disciples, "How hard it will be for those who have riches to enter the kingdom of God!"

²⁴ The disciples were amazed at his words. But Jesus told them again, "Children, how hard it is for those who trust in their riches to enter the kingdom of God! ²⁵ It is easier for a camel to go through the eye of a needle than for a rich man to enter the kingdom of God."

²⁶ They were even more astonished and said to one another, "Who then can be saved?" ²⁷ Jesus looked at them and said, "For people, it is impossible, but not for God, because all things are possible for God." ✠

The Gospel of our Lord. Praise be to you, O Christ!

---

[1] Exodus 20:12-16; Deuteronomy 5:16-20

Dear Friends in Christ Jesus:

Most people try to avoid extremes. Nobody likes it when the weather is too hot or too cold; we much prefer temperatures that are just right.

It's a general truism in politics that moderation is a good thing and that extremism is bad. In 1964, while he was running for president, Senator Barry Goldwater famously said: "Extremism in the defense of liberty is no vice! And ... moderation in the pursuit of justice is no virtue."[2] President Johnson's campaign quickly pounced on that quote. They painted Goldwater as an extremist who would lead us into nuclear war. Goldwater got clobbered in that election. Extremism scares people.

In spiritual matters it is also important to:

Beware of These Two Dangerous Extremes:

1) Overestimating Yourself, and
2) Underestimating God!

Part 1: First of All, Don't Overestimate Yourself!

In our Gospel lesson today, a young man ran up to Jesus and asked him:

Verse 17: *"Good teacher, what must I do to inherit eternal life?"*

The question itself reveals that this man was very mixed up. He had it in his head that he could attain eternal life by <u>doing</u> something on his own — by obeying some specific law or set of commands.

Notice that he called Jesus *"Good teacher."* He did not call him Lord or God or anything else that would indicate that he believed in Jesus as the Messiah, the Son of God. Listen to the way Jesus responded, as if to say: "Okay, so you want to qualify for eternal life? This is how you do it!" And then Jesus reminded him of the Second Table of the Law — that portion of God's Ten Commandments which demand that we love our neighbors just as we love ourselves.

---

[2] Barry Goldwater, in his acceptance speech as the 1964 Republican Presidential candidate.

<u>Verses 18-19</u>: *¹⁸ Jesus said to him, "Why do you call me good? No one is good except one — God. ¹⁹ You know the commandments. 'You shall not murder. You shall not commit adultery. You shall not steal. You shall not give false testimony. You shall not defraud. Honor your father and mother.'"*

When Jesus reminded him of God's holy Law, the rich man claimed that he had always obeyed all of these Commandments!

<u>Verse 20</u>: *The man replied, "Teacher, I have kept all these since I was a child."*

That young man was an extremist. He was extremely confident in himself. He thought he was able to qualify for heaven on his own — but he overestimated himself.

Jesus wanted to save the rich man's soul, so showed him that he had not even kept the First Commandment:

<u>Verse 21</u>: *Jesus looked at him, loved him, and said to him, "One thing you lack. Go, sell whatever you have, and give to the poor, and you will have treasure in heaven. Then come, follow me."*

Jesus was not suggesting that giving all your possessions to the poor is the way to heaven. He simply applied the First Commandment to this man: *"You shall have no other gods beside me."*[3] Jesus knew this young man's heart. He knew that this man's love of money was greater than his love for God.

<u>Verse 22</u>: *When he heard this, he looked sad and went away grieving, because he had great wealth.*

That man's love for his riches was greater than his love for God, and this proved his lack of faith. He trusted himself and his wealth rather than the Lord. The Ten Commandments teach us to love God most of all and to love our neighbor as we love ourselves; yet this rich man loved his riches more than he loved either God <u>or</u> his neighbor. He proved Jesus right when he walked away sad and grieving. He overestimated himself — a very dangerous extreme!

---

[3] Exodus 20:3

When you and I are comfortable in our sinful lives, or with our possessions, we need to hear God's holy Law. When you and I are comfortable with our own fine character and with what wonderful people we are, we need to hear God's holy Law. One of the main purposes of God's Law is to afflict the comfortable. When we are comfortable in overestimating ourselves and our own ability to please God, then we need to be reminded that God demands <u>perfect obedience</u> to his holy Law: <u>Love God</u> with every fiber of your being, <u>and love your neighbor</u> as you love yourself!

Now that's very bad news — bad, because none of us has kept all of God's Law perfectly. Bad, because we have not always loved God and his Commandments more than anyone or anything. Bad, because *"The wages of sin is death."*[4] Bad, because there is nothing we can do to change our situation. Love God most of all! That's very bad news. Bad, because we were conceived and born in sin, absolutely unable to please God in any way — unless God himself does something about our problem.

And praise God that he did! This is the <u>Good</u> News which comforts those who are afflicted by God's Law. He <u>did</u> do something about our plight! God <u>did</u> do something to change our situation! Our Heavenly Father sent his only-begotten Son Jesus into the flesh *"to destroy the works of the devil."*[5] He sent Jesus to pay the penalty for our countless sins. He sent Jesus to earn salvation for us, so that — sinners though we are — we inherit eternal life because of Jesus' saving work <u>for us</u>.

Which brings us to the other dangerous extreme: On the one hand, **Don't Overestimate Yourself!** And, on the other hand,

Part 2: Don't Underestimate God!

After the rich young man walked away sad and grieving,

<u>Verses 23-26</u>: *²³ Jesus looked around and said to his disciples, "How hard it will be for those who have riches to enter the kingdom of God!" ²⁴ The disciples were amazed at his words. But Jesus told them again, "Children, how hard it is*

---

[4] Romans 6:23
[5] 1 John 3:8

for those who trust in their riches to enter the kingdom of God! ²⁵ It is easier for a camel to go through the eye of a needle than for a rich man to enter the kingdom of God."

²⁶ They were even more astonished and said to one another, "Who then can be saved?"

Yes, Jesus' disciples were astonished. If this man could not earn his salvation, they figured, then who can? Do you see the danger? They underestimated God!

<u>Verse 27</u>: *Jesus looked at them and said, "For people, it is impossible, but not for God, because all things are possible for God."*

You see? With God, the impossible is possible!

Don't ever make this mistake. It's a dangerous extreme. God's people have often underestimated the Creator of the heavens and the earth.

- How could the Red Sea allow two million Children of Israel to walk right through it on dry land? With God, the impossible is possible! *"All things are possible for God."*

- How could all those people survive in the desert wilderness for forty years — along with their flocks and herds? With God, the impossible is possible! *"All things are possible for God."*

- How could Isaiah's prophesy that a virgin would conceive and bear a son come true? *"All things are possible for God."* The virgin Mary did bear a son whom we will always call Immanuel — God with us.

- How could Jesus calm the stormy sea simply by commanding it to be still? *"All things are possible for God."*

- How could Lazarus walk out of his tomb alive after being dead and embalmed for four days? *"All things are possible for God."*

- ☞ How could Jesus and his disciples feed five thousand men, plus women and children, with only five loaves of bread and two small fish — and have twelve baskets full of leftovers? *"All things are possible for God."*

- ☞ How could Jesus, after suffering and dying such a terrible, torturous execution, rise back to life from the dead two days later? *"All things are possible for God."*

Jesus said, *"For people, it is impossible, but not for God, because all things are possible for God."*

Our Lord suffered and died to pay for all those times when we <u>over</u>estimated ourselves, and for all of those times when we <u>under</u>estimated him. He is not only a man, but he is also true God — born of the virgin Mary, yet God's own Son from all eternity. He sacrificed his holy life for us, and by his death he paid for the sins of the world.

So **Don't Underestimate God** and his power to save! All things are possible with God. Never underestimate God's power to take good care of his people — especially when we are lonely, afraid, or afflicted with physical ailments or even financial trouble. Never underestimate God's power to save! *"All things are possible for God"* — even saving sinners the likes of you and me.

- ☞ God is so powerful that he can even create saving faith in the heart of a baby.

- ☞ He is so powerful that he can even convert hearts that are dead in sin into hearts that love and trust the Gospel of Jesus.

- ☞ He is so powerful that he can even take a very rich man, such as Abraham, and make a staunch believer out of him.

- ☞ If God wants to, he can even squeeze a camel through the eye of a needle.

- ☞ He is so powerful that he can heal every sickness, disease, and injury.

Our Lord can do anything he wants to do — and by his grace, he wants to save you and me! *"All things are possible for God!"* So let us never stop praising Almighty God for blessing us with faith in his crucified and risen Son Jesus, for washing away our sins in Baptism, for feeding our souls with the body and blood of Christ, and for blessing us with a precious inheritance in heaven — eternal life. In Jesus' holy name. AMEN.

The 22nd Sunday after Pentecost

TEXT: Hebrews 4:9-16

⁹ So there remains a Sabbath rest for the people of God. ¹⁰ For the one who enters God's rest also rests from his own work, just as God rested from his work. ¹¹ Therefore, let us make every effort to enter that rest, so that no one will fall into the same pattern of disobedience.

¹² For the word of God is living and active, sharper than any double-edged sword. It penetrates even to the point of dividing soul and spirit, joints and marrow, even being able to judge the ideas and thoughts of the heart. ¹³ And there is no creature hidden from him, but everything is uncovered and exposed to the eyes of him to whom we will give an account.

¹⁴ Therefore, since we have a great high priest who has gone through the heavens, namely, Jesus the Son of God, let us continue to hold on to our confession. ¹⁵ For we do not have a high priest who is unable to sympathize with our weaknesses, but one who has been tempted in every way, just as we are, yet was without sin. ¹⁶ So let us approach the throne of grace with confidence, so that we may receive mercy and find grace to help in time of need.

The Word of the Lord. Thanks be to God!

In the name of Jesus, our great High Priest, dear friends:

The Letter to the Hebrews is the only New Testament book whose authorship is unknown, so I will simply refer to the author as "the writer to the Hebrews." He was writing to Jewish Christians in and around Jerusalem sometime between A.D. 60 or 65 — just a few short years before the destruction of the Lord's temple by the Romans in A.D. 70. It was a time of terrible persecution of Christians by the leaders of the Jews.

The Hebrew Christians in Judea coincidence filled with fear on every side. What they needed was confidence — a stronger faith — and we need that, too. They needed to be reassured of God's grace and blessing — and so do we. So the Holy Spirit inspired this long and encouraging letter to motivate the Hebrew Christians to remain faithful to their Savior Jesus who had been so faithful to them. He gives many good reasons to be confident of God's mercy and grace.

He taught them and he teaches us that we can approach the throne of the Almighty without fear of being sent away, without fear of being zapped like bugs, without fear of being cast into hellfire. In verse 16 he encourages us, saying: *"Let us approach the throne of grace <u>with confidence</u>."* That's right!

God Gives Us Many Good Reasons to Be Confident!

First of all, we are:

Part 1: Confident That We Can Rest in Peace.

We often see headstones in cemeteries on which are engraved the three letters: "R.I.P." That stands for the Latin expression *Requiescat in pacem.* It's just a coincidence that the English translation "Rest in peace" has the same acronym.

Anyway, the writer to the Hebrews teaches that Jesus fulfilled the Old Testament ceremonial Law of Moses with all its regulations, and that Jesus did away with that law code for us New Testament Christians. For example, we don't have to worship God on Saturdays anymore. We are free to worship God on whatever day and at whatever time we freely choose. The Gospel gives us that freedom! But that doesn't mean that New Testament Christians don't get anymore rest just because the Sabbath Day command has been fulfilled and removed. Verse 9 assures us that *"There remains a Sabbath rest for the people of God."*

And what is that rest? It's the rest Jesus promised to all his people when he invited us to come to him, saying, *"Come to me, all you who are weary and burdened, and I will give you rest."*[1] The word *Sabbath* means "rest." Jesus was telling them: "You want rest? Come to <u>me</u>! <u>I</u> will give you Sabbath! <u>I</u> will give you rest!" And that's exactly what Jesus did for us when he died on the cross.

- ☞ <u>There</u> he fought the battle <u>for us</u> against our old evil Foe.
- ☞ <u>There</u> he poured out his lifeblood to appease the wrath of our Heavenly Father who was rightly and justly furious with us because of our countless sins.
- ☞ <u>There</u> on that cross Jesus established peace between God and man, just as the angels had promised: *"Peace on earth, good will towards men."*[2]

And now, because of what Jesus did <u>for us</u> and for the whole world, a Sabbath awaits us in the presence of our Creator. Now we can rest in peace, confident that our Savior gives true, eternal, spiritual rest, which is only found in his Word and Sacraments. The Gospel forgives all our sins and makes us confident that we <u>can</u> rest in peace — without fear, without worry, confident of the love of Jesus who cleanses us from all our sins.

Part 2: Yet Our Sins Do Not Escape God's Notice!

<u>Verse 12</u>: *The word of God is living and active, sharper than any double-edged sword. It penetrates even to the point of dividing soul and spirit, joints and marrow, even being able to judge the ideas and thoughts of the heart.*

Nothing escapes God's notice. God is well aware of our every thought, our every word, and our every deed.

<u>Verse 13</u>: *There is no creature hidden from him, but everything is uncovered and exposed to the eyes of him to whom we will give an account.*

This is a solemn reminder that God is deadly, eternally serious about sin — about all sins — including your sins and mine. St. Paul

---

[1] Matthew 11:28
[2] Luke 2:14

says that *"The wages of sin is death."*[3] That's what we get because we are sinners. You can be confident of that. Unless Jesus returns on clouds of glory first, we will all die — and we will all have to give an account of our sins to the Judge of all creation. Fortunately,

Part 3: We Can Be Confident, Because the Judge Is Also Our Great High Priest!

The writer to the Hebrews reminds us in:

<u>Verse 14</u>: *We have a great high priest who has gone through the heavens, namely, Jesus the Son of God.*

That's right! Jesus is our great High Priest! And what does every priest do? Every priest offers sacrifices to a holy God who is justly angry with his people because of their sins. Those sacrifices appease God and restore their relationship with him, so that once again God will bless his people rather than condemn them.

Jesus is our great High Priest. He offered up his life on the cross as the sacrifice which atones for the sins of all people. His resurrection from the grave proves that his Father accepted the sacrifice and that God is once again pleased with mankind.

Jesus promises in the last chapter of Mark's Gospel that *"Whoever believes and is baptized will be saved; whoever does not believe will be condemned."*[4] He makes that same promise in John's Gospel, that *"The one who believes in him is not condemned, but the one who does not believe is condemned already, because he has not believed in the name of the only-begotten Son of God."*[5]

Our great High Priest is one of us — 100% human. Yet, at the same time, he is 100% divine. Jesus is God and man in one person. And since he's a man, he's able to sympathize with our weaknesses.

<u>Verses 15-16</u>: *[15] We do not have a high priest who is unable to sympathize with our weaknesses, but one who has been tempted in every way, just as we are, yet was without sin. [16] So let us approach the throne of grace with confidence,*

---

[3] Romans 6:23
[4] Mark 16:16
[5] John 3:18

so that we may receive mercy and find grace to help in time of need.

Our High Priest knows exactly what it's like to be tempted. He was also tempted in every way, just as we are — though he never caved in to sin. So whenever we pray to our heavenly Father, we can always be confident that he will hear us and answer our prayers in the way he knows is best for us. We are his dear children, and he is our dear father. We will always find mercy at God's throne — after all, it <u>is</u> the throne of grace!

So my dear brothers and sisters, in Christ:

God Gives Us Many Good Reasons to Be Confident

— confident that we can rest in peace. And even though our sins do not escape God's notice, we can still be confident that the Judge of all mankind happens to be our great High Priest, Jesus Christ himself, the merciful Son of God, who died to pay for our sins and who rose back to life to declare us "not guilty!"

In the name of Jesus, our great High Priest. AMEN.

The 23rd Sunday after Pentecost

TEXT: Mark 10:46-52

⁴⁶ They came to Jericho. As Jesus and his disciples and a large crowd were leaving Jericho, a blind man, Bartimæus the son of Timæus, was sitting by the road begging. ⁴⁷ When he heard that it was Jesus the Nazarene, he began to shout, "Jesus, Son of David, have mercy on me!" ⁴⁸ Many told him to be quiet, but he kept shouting all the more, "Son of David, have mercy on me!"

⁴⁹ Jesus stopped and said, "Call him."

They called the blind man, saying, "Cheer up! Get up. He is calling you!"

⁵⁰ He tossed aside his outer garment, jumped up, and went to Jesus.

⁵¹ "What do you want me to do for you?" Jesus asked him.

The blind man replied, "Rabboni, I want to see again."

⁵² Jesus told him, "Go. Your faith has made you well." Immediately he received his sight and began following Jesus on the road. ✠

The Gospel of our Lord. Praise be to you, O Christ!

In the name of the Son of David, Jesus the Nazarene, dear friends:

There's a traditional Gospel song based on an old Negro spiritual. It's first line is: *"This little light of mine – I'm gonna let it shine!"* In Lutheran schools, one little word is usually added: *"This little Gospel light of mine — I'm gonna let it shine!"* After repeating the first line, it continues: *"Let it shine, all the time, let it shine!"*

The next stanza begins like this: *"All around the neighborhood I'm gonna let it shine!"* and so forth. We teach our children to sing this song¹, and others like it, to remind them of the importance of letting our light shine as we live our Christian faith.

In today's sermon text we learn about blind Bartimæus who publicly lived his faith in Jesus. He let his little Gospel light shine. And on the basis of these words in Mark chapter 10, I encourage you to do the same. Imitate Bartimæus as you:

Let Your Light Shine — By Living Your Faith!

Jesus and his disciples were walking south from the Galilee up to Jerusalem. St. Mark says in verse 46 that these events happened when they were near Jericho. Known as the City of Palms, Jericho boasted two beautiful oases in the desert where people and animals could always find a ready supply of clear water. It was customary for Galilean pilgrims to spend the night there before heading up the long and winding road to Jerusalem the next day.

Sitting along the side of the road was a blind beggar named Bartimæus. Though he looked poor on the outside, he was rich on the inside! He had never seen Jesus, of course, but he had heard plenty enough to know and believe that Jesus was his Savior. He had:

Part 1: Faith Which Knows Jesus.

How can we be so sure that blind Bartimæus trusted in Jesus as his Savior? Listen to:

Verses 47-48: *⁴⁷ When he heard that it was Jesus the Nazarene, he began to shout, "Jesus, Son of David, have mercy on me!" ⁴⁸ Many told him to be quiet, but he kept shouting all the more, "Son of David, have mercy on me!"*

The title "Son of David" was a technical term in Jewish theology. It was a Messianic title. When the blind man called Jesus the Son of David, he was calling him the Messiah. The Holy Spirit had worked faith in Bartimæus' heart that Jesus is the Christ, the Messiah whom God's prophets had foretold for thousands of years.

---

¹ An old African American spiritual in the public domain

Bartimæus was a man of faith, and he was not ashamed of his faith in the Son of David. Even when publicly rebuked by men who considered themselves his betters, this beggar gave bold testimony to the person of Jesus the Messiah.

Bartimæus let his Gospel light shine! What a wonderful example for Christians ever since. What a powerful example for *us*, too! No matter what the cost, no matter how much ridicule we may endure, we can also give bold testimony to our faith in Christ. We also know that Jesus is the Messiah, God's Son in human flesh, the Savior of the nations. We also know that Jesus is our Savior from sin, from death, and from the power of the Devil. By God's grace we know what Jesus has done for us and what he has done for the whole world. He sacrificed his life on the cross to atone for the sins of all people. And Jesus promises that everyone who believes and is baptized shall be saved. Grant this, O Lord, unto us all!

There are many ways that we can follow the example of Bartimæus:

- We can tell others the Good News of eternal life through the saving work of Jesus.
- We can join fellow Christians in spreading the Gospel in places where we may never go and among people we may never meet. That's what our church's mission programs are all about.
- We can remember to pray for the Holy Spirit to raise up many more faithful ministers of the Gospel to fill pulpits and classrooms and preach the Good News of Jesus to God's people.
- We can support these mission efforts with our offerings and with our prayers.
- And if we are told to be silent, we can continue proclaiming the Gospel of Jesus Christ, even in the face of ridicule and opposition.

Bartimæus had faith which knows Jesus, yet he also had:

Part 2: Faith Which Turns to Jesus.

Verse 49: *⁴⁹ Jesus stopped and said, "Call him."*

> They called the blind man, saying, "Cheer up! Get up. He is calling you!"

Bartimæus put his faith into practice. As soon as he heard that Jesus wanted him, he jumped at the opportunity.

<u>Verses 50-52</u>: > ⁵⁰*He tossed aside his outer garment, jumped up, and went to Jesus.*
>
> ⁵¹ *"What do you want me to do for you?" Jesus asked him.*
>
> *The blind man replied, "Rabboni, I want to see again."*
>
> ⁵² *Jesus told him, "Go. Your faith has made you well."*

His outer garment would have slowed him down, so he tossed it aside and took his petition straight to Jesus. Bartimæus called Jesus *Rabboni*, which was a Jewish title of respect for one's master teacher. Everything about these words testify to the sincerity of his faith in Jesus. So do Jesus' own words. After our Lord tells the blind man to *"Go,"* he says *"Your faith has made you well."* In all of this we see how Bartimæus let his light shine by turning to Jesus in faith. In fact, it was his God-given faith which moved him to turn to Jesus. He recognized Jesus as the One who fulfilled Isaiah's prophecy about the coming Messiah: *"The eyes of the blind will be opened."* [2] And he knew that Jesus alone had the power to heal his eyes. When Bartimæus took his prayer to Jesus, he was letting his little Gospel light shine.

We can also let our little Gospel light shine when we trusting Jesus to hear and answer our prayers. Other people see us living as Christian people. They see our approach to life and how we handle difficulties and troubles. They see us turn to Jesus in prayer — not only in times of crisis, but even when we're just saying "thank you" to God for his many blessings. People observe how we Christians deal with the deaths of our loved ones — and, for that matter, how we handle our own impending death.

Jesus promised to hear and answer our prayers, and our God-given faith moves us to take him up on his offer. In faith we turn to

---

[2] Isaiah 35:5

him just as Bartimæus did. He trusted in Jesus as the long-promised Savior, and that faith moved him to turn to Jesus for healing. Bartimæus let his light shine by following Jesus. How did that work out for him?

Verse 52:   *Immediately he received his sight and began following Jesus on the road.*

Dear brothers and sisters in Christ, Bartimæus is a wonderful example for us all.

Let Your Light Shine — by Living Your Faith
— faith which knows Jesus, faith which turns to Jesus, and
Part 3: Faith Which Follows Jesus.

Imagine how that blind man must have felt when suddenly he was able to see for the very first time! Out of gratitude he left his former life behind in order to follow Jesus. Our Lord had many disciples — many who followed to listen to his teachings, many who tagged along hoping to catch a glimpse of some miracle, and twelve men who had given up everything to follow Jesus full time in a life of service as apostles in the New Testament Church. We follow Bartimæus' example when we also follow Jesus as his disciples. People will see our little Gospel light shining.

Have you ever seen a little boy walking close behind his daddy, walking in his footsteps? That's how Jesus wants us to follow him in a life of Christian discipleship, with Christian values gleaned from a lifetime of studying his Word, letting our little Gospel light shine as we walk with him in faith.

The Holy Spirit has kindled in your heart the flame of faith. *"Hide it under a bushel? No! ... I'm gonna let it shine!"* — just as Bartimæus did.

It is well said that the light which shines the farthest out into the darkness is the light which shines brightest at its base. To make our own little Gospel light shine brighter and farther, it's crucial that we faithfully attend the worship services of God's house, regularly and often feeding on the Gospel of Jesus in his holy Word and Sacraments. In order to shine our little Gospel light more and more brightly into this sin-darkened world, let us spend more and more time studying our Bibles, learning from our Master Teacher, so that we can follow Jesus as his disciples. May God bless you with the example of Bartimæus!

Let Your Light Shine — by Living Your Faith.

But this section Holy Scripture is much more about the One who did the healing than about the man who was healed. It's about Jesus! How could Jesus give sight to the blind — or perform <u>any</u> miracles, for that matter? Only God can do miracles. Jesus did miracles. Therefore, Jesus is God. And what an amazing God we have! He entered his own creation and became a human being, just like you and I. He sacrificed his life on Calvary's cross to atone for our countless sins. And this God-man Jesus rose back to life from the dead as our victorious Savior. Before he returned to his home above, he promised: *"Whoever believes and is baptized will be saved, but whoever does not believe will be condemned."*[3]

This is the faith which the Holy Spirit created in the heart of blind Bartimæus. It's the same faith he created in your heart and in mine.

Let Your Light Shine — by Living Your Faith

— just as blind Bartimæus did.

> *This little Gospel light of mine —*
> *I'm gonna let it shine,*
> *Let it shine, all the time, let it shine!*

AMEN.

---

[3] Mark 16:16

The 24th Sunday after Pentecost

TEXT: Mark 12:28-34

²⁸ One of the experts in the law approached after he heard their discussion. When he saw that Jesus had answered them well, he asked Jesus, "Which commandment is the greatest of all?"

²⁹ Jesus answered, "The most important is: 'Hear, O Israel, the Lord, our God, the Lord is one. ³⁰ You shall love the Lord your God with all your heart, with all your soul, with all your mind, and with all your strength.'[1] ³¹ The second is this: 'You shall love your neighbor as yourself.'[2] There is no other commandment greater than these."

³² The expert in the law said to him, "Well said, teacher. You have spoken correctly on the basis of the truth that he is one, and there is no other besides him.[3] ³³ To love him with all your heart, with all your understanding, and with all your strength, and to love your neighbor as yourself, is more important than all whole burnt offerings and sacrifices."[4]

³⁴ When Jesus saw that he had answered wisely, he said to him, "You are not far from the kingdom of God." After that, no one dared to ask him any more questions. ✠

The Gospel of our Lord. Praise be to you, O Christ!

In the name of Jesus, who <u>is</u> Perfect Love in human flesh, dear friends:

What is love? The great thinkers and star struck lovers of this world have been struggling with that question for many centuries.

---

[1] Deuteronomy 6:4-5

[2] Leviticus 19:18

[3] Deuteronomy 6:4; 4:35; Isaiah 45:21

[4] Deuteronomy 6:5; Leviticus 19:18

The Pentecost Season

Since the Holy Spirit inspired the New Testament to be written in Greek, it is instructive to know that there are at least eight different words for love in the Greek language, but only three of those words appear in the Bible:

Cháris (χάρις) = God's undeserved love for sinners, love which seeks our salvation. Only God can have this kind of love!

Agápē (ἀγάπη) = Self-sacrificing love which only seeks the benefit of the object of one's affection, regardless of whether or not you're going to receive anything in return. This is the kind of love we Christians have for each other and that Christ has for us.

Philía (φιλία) = Very strong friendship or brotherly love.

In a world where people are searching for answers to life's deepest questions, and in a world where people so often look for love in all the wrong places, we turn to God's Word today and see in this text that:

Perfect Love Is the Perfect Answer
1) To a Most Important Question;
2) To a Most Dreadful Dilemma; and
3) To a Most Precious Opportunity.

It was Tuesday of Holy Week — often called "Busy Tuesday" for Jesus. A few days later would be Good Friday. In Jerusalem he was being questioned by many who only wanted to entrap him — first the Pharisees, then the Herodians, and finally the Sadducees. A scribe, that is, as our text calls him, *"one of the experts in the law,"* wanted an answer from Jesus, the Master Rabbi:

Part 1: To a Most Important Question

"Which commandment is the greatest of all?" Knowing the correct answer to that question is very, very important! This highly trained Jewish theologian was asking of Jesus something commonly asked of respected rabbis. After all, the Law of Moses contains 613 individual commands. There's no way that the average person could remember every single one of them, much less obey every single one of them perfectly all the time. So if you don't want to get shut out of

heaven by violating the one commandment about which God is most concerned, you'd better know what that most important commandment is! That Jewish scholar wanted to be sure that *he* would measure up to God's requirements.

That's a very important question for us, too! Nature itself testifies to the existence of God, who is an all-powerful and all-knowing divine Being. Our conscience also testifies to God's existence and that we will have to answer to him some day for our actions in this life. But what if you failed to obey the one commandment that the divine Judge considers to be the most important one of all? Wouldn't you like to know what that is in advance, so that you can be certain to fulfill that commandment before the Day comes when you must stand before his Judgment?

"Which commandment is the greatest of all?" the scholar asks. Now listen to Jesus' response, which leads:

Part 2: To a Most Dreadful Dilemma.

Verses 29-31: *²⁹ Jesus answered, "The most important is: 'Hear, O Israel, the Lord, our God, the Lord is one. ³⁰ You shall love the Lord your God with all your heart, with all your soul, with all your mind, and with all your strength.'*[5] *³¹ The second is this: 'You shall love your neighbor as yourself.'*[6] *There is no other commandment greater than these."*

Jesus answers by quoting directly from the Law. Moses says: "All ... all ... all ... all...." *"You shall love the Lord your God with all your heart, with all your soul, with all your mind, and with all your strength."* And that Greek verb which the Holy Spirit inspired St. Mark to use here when reporting Jesus' words for us is *agapáō* (ἀγαπάω) = Love! God requires us to love him with all our heart, with all our soul, with all our mind, and with all our strength. And that's not optional. God demands it! Loving God most of all is the greatest and most important commandment of all.

---

[5] Deuteronomy 6:4-5

[6] Leviticus 19:18

Jesus goes on to tell this expert in the Law the second greatest commandment: *'You shall love your neighbor as yourself.'* And Jesus concludes: *"There is no other commandment greater than these."*

Therein lies our most dreadful dilemma. God demands perfect love! We must love him perfectly, at all times. If we don't, we become law breakers. We must love our fellow human beings just as much as we love ourselves, at all times. If we don't, we become law breakers. Our dilemma is simply this: Who among us has always loved God and always loved his neighbor perfectly? St. John says:

<u>1 John 4:20</u>: *If anyone says, "I love God," but hates his brother, he is a liar. For how can anyone who does not love his brother, whom he has seen, love God, whom he has not seen?*

Jesus gives a perfectly good answer to a perfectly good question, but the answer leaves us with a dreadful dilemma. If we have not loved God perfectly, and we have not loved our neighbor perfectly, how can we stand before the Almighty on Judgment Day? What can we do? That's our dreadful dilemma. We're all doomed! We need a Savior!

But praise God from whom all blessings flow! *God <u>is</u> love!*[7] Our Heavenly Father has given his only-begotten Son to be the Savior we all need. He showed his undeserved, self-sacrificing love to us by sending Jesus to rescue us from the eternal consequences of our sins. God provided the perfect answer to our dreadful dilemma by giving us the perfect love of Jesus. How much does he love us? He spread his arms wide and allowed those soldiers to nail his body to a cross in order to atone for our sins. His perfect self-sacrificing love is God's answer to our dreadful dilemma. It is also his answer:

Part 3: To a Most Precious Opportunity

<u>Verses 32-33</u>: *[32] The expert in the law said to him, "Well said, teacher. You have spoken correctly on the basis of the*

---

[7] 1 John 4:8 and 16

truth that he is one, and there is no other besides him. [8]
³³ To love him with all your heart, with all your understanding, and with all your strength, and to love your neighbor as yourself, is more important than all whole burnt offerings and sacrifices." [9]

The scribe's evaluation of God's perfect Law of perfect love was correct! He correctly understood God's holy Law. But listen to Jesus' evaluation of that expert in the Law in:

<u>Verse 34</u>: *When Jesus saw that he had answered wisely, he said to him, "You are not far from the kingdom of God."*

The sad truth is that *"not far"* means that you're still not quite there yet, Mister Scribe! You may be standing only an inch away from the pool, but you're still bone dry. A one inch miss is as good as a mile.

You see, that expert in the Law understood God's Law very well, but he was no expert in the Gospel! He did not grasp the Good News of God's free and faithful grace. Yet Jesus' answer should keep him searching, for Jesus says that he's *"not far from the kingdom of God."* He shouldn't need to search very far. Three days from now he'll see Jesus arrested and beaten, tried and condemned, scourged, crucified, and buried. All of this Jesus would suffer in order to give his perfect love to that scribe, to you, to me, and to the whole world.

So when the world looks at <u>us</u>, what do they think? Do they know that we are God's children, true disciples of Jesus? Our Savior says: *"By this everyone will know that you are my disciples, if you have love for one another."* [10] You see,

Perfect Love is the Perfect Answer!

May it <u>never</u> be said that <u>we</u> *"are not far from the kingdom of God."* Rather, may it always be said that we are certainly in it! AMEN.

---

[8] Deuteronomy 6:4; 4:35; Isaiah 45:21

[9] Deuteronomy 6:5; Leviticus 19:18

[10] John 13:35

The 25th Sunday after Pentecost

TEXT: Hebrews 9:24-28

²⁴ Christ did not enter a handmade sanctuary, a representation of the true sanctuary. Instead, he entered into heaven itself, now to appear before God on our behalf. ²⁵ And he did not enter to offer himself many times, as the high priest enters the Most Holy Place year after year with blood that is not his own. ²⁶ Otherwise he would have needed to suffer many times since the creation of the world. But now he has appeared once and for all, at the climax of the ages, in order to take away sin by the sacrifice of himself. ²⁷ And, just as it is appointed for people to die only once and after this comes the judgment, ²⁸ so also Christ was offered only once to take away the sins of many, and he will appear a second time — without sin — to bring salvation to those who are eagerly waiting for him. ✠

The Word of the Lord. Thanks be to God!

In the name of Jesus, our Great High Priest, dear friends:

There was a <u>lot</u> of persecution of Christians in and around Jerusalem, Judea, and the Galilee when the Holy Spirit inspired the writer to the Hebrews. This New Testament letter was written just a few years before the Romans destroyed the temple in A.D. 70 — probably in the mid-60s. The Hebrew Christians were Jewish by blood, but they had been converted to faith in Jesus as the Messiah, so they were persecuted for their Christian faith. It was a big temptation for them to forget that they had ever heard of Jesus. Their path of least resistance would have been to go back to being faithful Jews.

This letter encourages those Hebrew Christians to hang in there. Don't give up your faith! Don't let go of your Christianity! Why not? The writer to the Hebrews gives them — and he gives <u>us</u> — some very excellent reasons to remain faithful to Jesus:

- First of all, the greatest prophet of the Jews was Moses, but our Lord Jesus is a far greater Prophet even than Moses!
- Secondly, Jesus is far greater than all the angels. God created the angels to serve Jesus and us!
- And thirdly,

Our **High Priest is the Greatest Priest of All!**

Let's unpack these verses and see what God is teaching us today.

<u>Verse 24</u>: *Christ did not enter a handmade sanctuary, a representation of the true sanctuary. Instead, he entered into heaven itself, now to appear before God on our behalf.*

First of all, Jewish high priests functioned in a man-made sanctuary at Jerusalem. Jesus performed his priestly duties in the greatest sanctuary of all: heaven itself! The temple at Jerusalem was gorgeous. Its artwork and architecture were absolutely grand; yet God's temple at Jerusalem was merely a representation of the sanctuary in heaven. Jewish priests functioned in the handmade representation, but Jesus performed his priesthood in the real thing!

<u>Verses 25-26</u>: *^{25} And he did not enter to offer himself many times, as the high priest enters the Most Holy Place year after year with blood that is not his own. ^{26} Otherwise he would have needed to suffer many times since the creation of the world. But now he has appeared once and for all....*

Secondly, Jewish high priests had to repeat their sacrifices many times, over and over and over. Animals had to be sacrificed over and over and over. The animal sacrifices which the priests offered in the temple Jerusalem never really paid for any sins. They merely taught God's people that without the shedding of blood there is no payment for sin. Somebody had to atone for the sins of mankind, and priests who sacrificed mere animals could not do the job. They could not do what Jesus did! He performed <u>his</u> sacrifice once and for all. One and done. Jesus' sacrifice made all other sacrifices obsolete!

<u>Verses 26 & 28</u>: *^{26} [Jesus] has appeared once and for all, at the climax of the ages, in order to take away sin by the sacri-*

fice of himself. ... ²⁸ Christ was offered only once to take away the sins of many....

This brings up the third reason why Jesus is far superior to the Jewish high priests. Those priests had to offer to God blood which was not their own. Bulls and heifers, sheep and goats, doves and pigeons, etc. — they all spilled their blood in a vain attempt to satisfy God's anger over the sins of his people, but to no avail. The animals certainly had nothing to say about it. If any priest ever spilled any blood while offering a sacrifice, it was only an accident when cutting up the animal!

But Jesus was the only priest who ever sacrificed himself. He willing obeyed his Father's will and poured out his own precious blood on the tree of the cross in order to cover over the sins of the world. Jesus demonstrated his self-sacrificing love for us sinners best when he offered up his life for us. He gave himself as the only sacrifice which could atone for our sins and for the sins of the whole human race.

The entire history of this universe is centered around one event: Jesus *"has appeared once and for all, at the climax of the ages."* Beginning with Moses' account of creation, the entire Old Testament pointed forward to Jesus. Ever since Adam and Eve chose to sin, God sent a long line of prophets to tell his people what he was going to do about it. He was going to send his own Son into human flesh, the Seed of a woman, and he would destroy the devil's work. God promised that the Seed would be a descendent of Abraham, Isaac, Jacob, and Judah. God promised that he would descend from King David and reign on his throne forever. And through his Old Testament prophets, God gave his people many more details about the coming Messiah.

And in his own good time, God kept all of his promises and gave his Son Jesus to rescue the world from damnation. St. John says it this way:

<u>John 3:16-18</u>: *¹⁶ God so loved the world that he gave his only-begotten Son, that whoever believes in him shall not perish, but have eternal life. ¹⁷ For God did not send his Son into the world to condemn the world, but to save the world through him. ¹⁸ The one who believes in him is not con-*

demned, but the one who does not believe is condemned already, because he has not believed in the name of the only-begotten Son of God.

Ever since the life and death, resurrection and ascension of our great High Priest Jesus, we have been living post-climax. God has sent his apostles and evangelists, his pastors and teachers, to proclaim the very same messages which were preached by the prophets of the Old Testament — but now we point <u>backwards</u> in time to the climax of the ages which already happened about two thousand years ago. Today's ministers of the Gospel remind you of what Jesus did for you.

God did indeed enter human flesh. He offered that one sacrifice which God required for your salvation. He rose back to life from the dead because he is God, and God can do that! He controls all matters of life and death. Forty days later he returned to heaven, promising to prepare a place for us, promising to come back in judgment someday, and promising to take us with him to heaven.

<u>Verses 27-28</u>: *[27] Just as it is appointed for people to die only once and after this comes the judgment, [28] so also Christ was offered only once to take away the sins of many, and he will appear a second time — without sin — to bring salvation to those who are eagerly waiting for him.*

These are the reasons we need to be faithful to our faithful God:

- Jesus is our great high priest who atoned for our sins by laying down his life for us, offering his body and blood on the cross.

- He offered that sacrifice once, and only once, and that one sacrifice counts for all the sins of all people of all time.

- God the Father was so pleased with the perfect sacrifice Jesus offered for us that he raised his Son back to life from the dead.

- So we do not worship a dead martyr. We do not need the ministry of any human priests. We only need Jesus, who is the greatest high priest of all.

So don't let go of your Christian faith! Hang on to Jesus! Never give up hope in Christ! Trust in him alone for forgiveness and salvation! After all, Jesus is the One who will return in glory to save you from damnation on Judgment Day. To him alone be all the glory! AMEN.

The 26th Sunday after Pentecost

TEXT: Daniel 12:1-4

¹ Then at that time, Michael, the great prince who stands over your people, will arise. There will be a time of distress that has not happened from the first time that there was a nation until that time.

At that time your people will be delivered, everyone who is found written in the book. ² Many who are sleeping in the dusty ground will awake, some to everlasting life, and some to shame, to everlasting contempt. ³ Those who have insight will shine like the brightness of the sky, and those who bring many to righteousness will shine like the stars forever and ever. ⁴ Now you, Daniel, close up the words and seal the scroll until the time of the end. Many will continue running back and forth, and knowledge will increase. ✠

The Word of the Lord. Thanks be to God!

In Christ Jesus, dear friends:

Most people want to excel at whatever they do. Some want to do just enough to get by, but most people figure that anything worth doing is worth doing right and worth doing well. Most athletes hope to become good enough in their sport that they get named to the All Star team.

I don't see many professional athletes out there! I do see a few high school athletes, and a few adult weekend warriors — but I doubt whether many of you been named All Stars. If you have, good for you! But if you have not, someday you and I and all of God's faithful people will be named to God's All Star Team!

How do we know that this is really true? Because God told Daniel to write this down for you and me to know, and for us to believe! One day, we will each:

Shine Like an All Star!

Daniel was not technically a "prophet." He was an administrator. He was a Jew working for the Persian government. Nevertheless, God inspired Daniel to write down his prophetic words for the benefit of his Old Testament people — and for us.

Daniel was just a boy when the Babylonians took him — along with 90% of the Jews away from Jerusalem and the surrounding territory of Judah — into what became known as the Babylonian captivity. There in Babylon Daniel received an excellent education and was pressed into the service of the king. He did such a fine job and was so faithful that the king made him a high ranking government official. But then the Persians took over, and the Neo-Babylonian empire was no more. Since Daniel was not an ethnic Babylonian (in fact, he was a Jew), and because he was such an excellent and faithful administrator, the Persian king made Daniel governor of a huge territory in his empire. He served the kings of Persia for the rest of his life.

This section of the Book of Daniel deals with prophecy about the end times — about these last days between Pentecost and Christ's return on Judgment Day. There is nothing scary here! God makes no threats here. He only gives Daniel information to convey to us and he gives us many reasons to rejoice.

So <u>rejoice</u>, dear brothers and sisters! <u>Rejoice</u> — because:

Part 1: Your Name Is Written in the Book of Life!

<u>Verse 1</u>:   *Then at that time, Michael, the great prince who stands over your people, will arise. There will be a time of distress that has not happened from the first time that there was a nation until that time.*

At that time your people will be delivered, everyone who is found written in the book.

Who is Michael? He is one of only two of God's angels mentioned by name in the Bible. Michael is the angel who obeys God's command to rescue his faithful people and destroy the devil. Michael is the archangel who, in these last days, is leading many of God's holy angels in victorious conflict against Satan and his minions. Michael is constantly protecting all of God's people during this time of great distress — a time when Satan runs wild on this earth and evil knows no bounds — a time of tribulation which will only come to an end when the Son of God returns on clouds of glory for the final judgment, when he will cast Satan and his evil angels into the eternal lake of fire.

Daniel calls the people of God *"everyone who is found written in the book."* He is talking about the Book of Life. King David speaks about that book in Psalm 69:28, when he calls down a curse upon God's enemies, saying, *"May they be erased from the book of life."*

In the book of Revelation St. John tells us what he saw in his vision of Judgment Day. John says:

> *I saw the dead, great and small, standing before the throne, and books were opened. Another book was opened, which is the book of life. The dead were judged according to what they had done as recorded in the books.* [1]
>
> *If anyone's name was not found written in the book of life, he was thrown into the lake of fire.* [2]
>
> *Nothing impure will ever enter it, nor will anyone who does what is shameful or deceitful, but only those whose names are written in the Lamb's book of life.* [3]

Do you know whose names are written in the Book of Life? Your name is in there! So is the name of everyone who believes the Gospel and is baptized. Jesus died to pay for all the sins of all the people who have ever lived in this world, and for the sins of everyone who ever <u>will</u> live in this world. Sadly, not everyone believes the Gospel of Jesus Christ and not everyone has been baptized, so their names are not found in that Book.

But you don't need to worry about whether or not your name is in there. Rejoice that your name <u>is</u> written in the Lamb's Book of Life! And rejoice that:

Part 2: You Will Rise from the Dead!

---

[1] Revelation 20:12

[2] Revelation 20:15

[3] Revelation 21:27

The 27ᵗʰ Sunday after Pentecost

TEXT: Malachi 4:1-6

¹ "Look! The day is coming, burning like a blast furnace. All the arrogant and every evildoer will be stubble. The day that is coming will set them on fire, says the LORD of Armies, a day that will not leave behind a root or branch for them. ² But for you who fear my name, the sun of righteousness will rise, and there will be healing in its wings. You will go out and jump around like calves from the stall. ³ You will trample the wicked. They will surely be ashes under the soles of your feet on the day when I take action, says the LORD of Armies.

⁴ "Remember the law of my servant Moses, which I commanded to him at Horeb to serve as statutes and judgments over all Israel.

⁵ "Look! I am going to send Elijah the prophet to you before the great and fearful day of the LORD comes! ⁶ He will turn the hearts of fathers to their children and the hearts of children to their fathers. Otherwise, I will come and strike the land with complete destruction." ✡

The Word of the Lord. Thanks be to God!

In the name of Jesus, the Sun of Righteousness himself, dear Christian friends:

Did you ever notice that most Christian churches are built in such a manner that the congregation faces the east, in expectation of the rising sun? (Not all, but most.) Synagogues are usually laid out in the same manner, with their congregations facing the east. This is because of the pun (the play on words) found in this text from Malachi's pen. We, the people of God, wait in eager anticipation of the rising of the sun — God's one and only Son, Jesus Christ!

The Sun of Righteousness Will Rise!

Malachi wrote to God's people a little more than a century after their ancestors had returned from seventy years of captivity in Babylon. They had struggled mightily to rebuild Jerusalem and the LORD's temple. The Holy Spirit inspired Malachi to write these words about 400 B.C. What had they learned in captivity? Had they learned to be faithful to the LORD? Well, for the first few decades after their great grandparents returned, they were generally faithful. They observed the Sabbath every week, the Passover every spring, and all the other annual festivals prescribed by Moses. They stayed away from their gentile neighbors and remained a people dedicated to God. By and large they brought their tithes and offerings faithfully to God's rebuilt house.

But just a couple of generations later, God's people were back to their old tricks. Rather than worshipping God every Sabbath day, they were working — though in his Third Commandment God had strictly forbidden them to work on the Sabbath. They were ignoring the worship rituals prescribed by the Law of Moses. They intermarried with their heathen Gentile neighbors, and they divorced their faithful spouses. God's chosen people were not joyfully bringing their offerings to God's house, and the priests were not faithfully teaching God's Word.

So God gave them one last warning of his impending judgment and one final promise of his salvation — all wrapped up into this final chapter of the Old Testament. For the next four centuries, God would not send them any more messages, nor any more prophets. God's Word would be very scarce until the arrival of John the Baptist. John would fulfil God's promise to send Elijah:

Verse 5: *Look! I am going to send Elijah the prophet to you before the great and fearful day of the LORD comes!*

And when John came four centuries later, he preached the same message that Elijah and Malachi and all of God's faithful prophets had proclaimed: *"Repent, because the kingdom of heaven is near!"*[1]

Part 1: Judgment Day Is Surely Coming Soon!

Jesus says to his disciples:

---

[1] Matthew 3:2

<u>Verse 1</u>: *Look! The day is coming, burning like a blast furnace.*

The coming Day of the LORD was repeatedly foretold by God and his prophets throughout the Old Testament, and was repeatedly promised by Jesus and by St. Peter in the New. In 2nd Peter chapter three the Apostle gives us many specifics about the last days leading up to the return of Christ. He says:

> ☞ *In the last days scoffers will come with their mocking, following their own lusts. ... They will say, "Where is this promised coming of his?" ... What they intentionally forget is that the former world perished when it was flooded with water.*

> ☞ *The heavens and earth have been stored up for fire, since they are being kept until the day of judgment and the destruction of the ungodly.*

> ☞ *The Lord ... is patient, not wanting anyone to perish, but all to come to repentance.*

> ☞ *The day of the Lord will come like a thief. ... The heavens will pass away with a roar, the elements will be dissolved as they burn with great heat, and the earth and what was done on it will be burned up.* [2]

Jesus promised that he would return soon. Now here we are, two thousand years later, and Christ has not yet returned. Those who don't believe Jesus say that he was lying when he foretold his return for judgment, so there's no need for anyone to be concerned about it, they say.

But the <u>real</u> reason the wicked scoff at the promise of Christ's immanent return is that, if they acknowledge that there will be a Day of Judgment, they will have to change their wicked ways — which they refuse to do. And if they <u>don't</u> repent of their wicked ways and turn to Jesus for forgiveness and salvation, they will have to spend eternity in hell — the existence of which they deny. The wicked are, after all, unbelievers, and their denial of the clear teachings of God's Word is proof of their wickedness!

---

[2] 2 Peter 3:3-10

Part 2: When Judgment Day <u>Does</u> Come, the Wicked Will Be Burned like Stubble!

Verse 1: *All the arrogant and every evildoer will be stubble. The day that is coming will set them on fire, says the LORD of Armies, a day that will not leave behind a root or branch for them.*

Jesus taught about a man burning in hell. Remember the Rich Man and Poor Lazarus? [3] When the rich man went to hell, he appealed to Father Abraham in heaven to send Lazarus down from heaven with a little water to relieve his misery. Abraham reminded him that he had had his chances while he was alive in this world, but he had blown it. Abraham told him that there's a great chasm fixed between heaven and hell so that it's impossible for anyone to cross over in either direction. Abraham concluded the conversation by saying that people who are still alive in this world need to pay heed *"to Moses and the prophets,"* and that if they refuse to listen to them, they won't believe even if someone rises from the dead. And even though Jesus did exactly that, most people in this world still refuse to listen to his Word and believe. But:

Part 3: When Judgment Day <u>Does</u> Arrive, God's Faithful People Will Rejoice!

Verse 2: *But for you who fear my name, the sun of righteousness will rise, and there will be healing in its wings. You will go out and jump around like calves from the stall.*

This prophecy of Jesus contains a pun — a play on words — a pun that works just as well in English as it does in Malachi's own Hebrew. That *sun of righteousness* is Jesus, the perfectly righteous Son of God. He will rise for the benefit of all *who fear* his *name.*

Just as surly as the sun rises every day, Jesus, the *"sun of righteousness,"* came into this world of sinners. He came, as St. Paul says, *"When the set time had fully come."*[4] God had set his own time on his own calendar, and his timing, as always, was perfect. God led the affairs of men and of nations to just exactly the right point in

---

[3] Luke 16:19-31

[4] Galatians 4:4

history when all of the prophecies about the coming Messiah would be fulfilled. God's only-begotten Son, the *sun of righteousness*, came into this world with *healing in its wings.* For over three years he walked around the Holy Land, preaching, teaching, and healing every disease and sickness. By living a perfectly righteous life, he established the perfect righteousness that God demands of all people. By his innocent suffering and death, *the sun of righteousness* paid the debt we owed to our holy God for all of our unrighteous thoughts, words, and deeds. Then Jesus rose back to life with *healing in* his *wings* in order to heal our sin-sickened souls. His life and death paid our debt in full, and he promises eternal life to all who trust him in for salvation.

Since Jesus has promised us eternal life in heaven, we rejoice just as calves who have been released from their stalls. They jump around while enjoying their freedom, and we rejoice in the freedom God has given us:

- freedom from slavery to sin and Satan,
- freedom from the fear of death,
- freedom to love and serve and worship God without the shackles of the Old Testament ceremonial laws,
- and freedom to love and serve our fellow human beings as a reflection of Jesus' love for us.

We live in a wicked world. We like to think of our country as a Christian nation, though it's very hard to draw that conclusion when we watch the evening news, or read the morning paper, or observe the fact that fewer than 20% of the citizens of this great nation are worshiping God in any Christian church on any given weekend.

And to be fair, we have contributed to the problem ourselves! Our own weaknesses, our own shortcomings, and our own sins have contributed to the problems of our society; so let's not point our fingers at others until we honestly confront our own sinfulness. Let us not concern ourselves with the splinters in our neighbors' eyes when we have logs in our own eyes. The best way to begin cleaning up the social ills in our community and in our country is to clean up our own act. By that I mean turning to Jesus, *the sun of righteousness*, repenting of our own sins, and finding the *healing in* his *wings.*

The Day is surely drawing near! The Day is coming when the cup of this world's iniquity will be full, when God will have had enough of the sins of men, when God will say, "That's it!" With no more warning than he has already given in the Scriptures, he will send his angels to blow the final trumpet, and Jesus will gather every human being, dead <u>and</u> alive, before his judgment seat. There will be no avoiding God's judgment, no excuses, no lies — only honest confession that Jesus Christ is Lord, to the glory of God the Father.

Listen once again to verses 1 and 2. This is a message which cannot be proclaimed or heard too often:

<u>Verses 1-2</u>: *¹All the arrogant and every evildoer will be stubble. The day that is coming will set them on fire, says the LORD of Armies, a day that will not leave behind a root or branch for them. ² But for you who fear my name, the sun of righteousness will rise, and there will be healing in its wings.*

What a terrible comeuppance that Day will be for every arrogant evildoer, for everyone who does not trust in *the sun of righteousness.* They will find no *healing in its wings.* But what a wonderful Day that will be for <u>us</u> who <u>do</u> fear his name, who <u>do</u> eagerly await his return in glory, for we will be clothed in the robes of Christ's righteousness and ushered to our reserved seats at the eternal wedding feast of the Lamb.

Thank you, Lord Jesus, for atoning for our sins! Thank you, O Lord, for promising unconditional forgiveness and eternal life to all who believe! Thank you for washing away our sins in Holy Baptism and making us children of the Heavenly Father! Thank you for strengthening our faith regularly and often through your Holy Word! Thank you for nourishing our souls regularly and often with your body and blood in Holy Communion! And thank you for the fellowship we enjoy with all your faithful people who fear your holy name!

To God alone be all the glory! AMEN.

Michaelmas: The Feast of St. Michael and All Angels

(September 29, or the last Sunday in September)

TEXT: Matthew 18:1-11

¹ *At that time the disciples approached Jesus and asked, "Who then is the greatest in the kingdom of heaven?"*

² *Jesus called a little child, had him stand in the middle of them, ³ and said, "Amen I tell you: Unless you are turned and become like children, you will never enter the kingdom of heaven. ⁴ Whoever humbles himself like this little child is the greatest in the kingdom of heaven. ⁵ And whoever receives a little child like this one in my name receives me.*

⁶ *"But, if anyone causes one of these little ones who believe in me to sin, it would be better for him to have a huge millstone hung around his neck and to be drowned in the depths of the sea. ⁷ Woe to the world because of temptations to sin. Temptations must come, but woe to that person through whom the temptation comes!*

⁸ *"If your hand or your foot causes you to sin, cut it off and throw it away. It is better for you to enter life crippled or lame than to be thrown into the eternal fire with two hands or two feet. ⁹ If your eye causes you to sin, pluck it out and throw it away from you. It is better for you to enter life with one eye than to be thrown into hell fire with two eyes. ¹⁰ See to it that you do not look down on one of these little ones, because I tell you that their angels in heaven always see the face of my Father who is in heaven. ¹¹ For the Son of Man came to save what was lost."* ✠

The Gospel of our Lord. Praise be to you, O Christ!

In the name of Jesus, the Friend of Sinners and especially of children, dear fellow children of God:

Jesus' twelve closest disciples were constantly arguing among themselves for primacy. Which one of them would be number one in the Kingdom of Heaven? Who would be number two? After all, Jesus kept preaching and teaching that he was going to establish God's Kingdom, and they were his closest friends and allies. It only stood to reason that they would be the top officials in this new government, right? The way they figured, that would bring them lots of prestige and power. Since they had all left their former occupations to follow Jesus in a life of full-time discipleship, they expected to remain in his inner circle when he set up his Kingdom. But who among them would have the greatest honor? Who would be the "top dog"? What would the pecking order be?

Jesus knew that they had a lot to learn about servant-leadership, and that they would never learn these things by observing worldly kingdoms. So he kept teaching them very important concepts that apply in the Kingdom of Heaven and in his holy Christian Church.

You see, what those Twelve needed was the same thing that we and all Christians need:

A Simple, Child-like Faith

St. Matthew reports to us in Chapter 18 that, one day:

Verses 1-3: *¹ The disciples approached Jesus and asked, "Who then is the greatest in the kingdom of heaven?" ² Jesus called a little child, had him stand in the middle of them, ³ and said, "Amen I tell you: Unless you are turned and become like children, you will never enter the kingdom of heaven."*

Now whenever Jesus begins a sentence with the word "Amen," he is saying: "Pay very careful attention to what I am about to say; this is particularly important!" So when he takes a little child and places him in front of them as an object lesson, Jesus says: *"Amen I tell you: Unless you are turned and become like children, you will never enter the kingdom of heaven."* Jesus was teaching the Twelve something very important! He was teaching the Twelve — and he is teaching us that:

A Simple, Child-like Faith
Part 1: Is Humble Before Almighty God.

Our Lord Jesus says in:

Verse 4: *"Whoever humbles himself like this little child is the greatest in the kingdom of heaven."*

That little child standing in the middle of Jesus and his disciples knew that everyone around him was bigger, stronger, more experienced, and more knowledgeable than he was. He had every reason to be humble before them! Jesus teaches us that we are to be just as humble as that little child.

Now admittedly, humbling ourselves is not a natural thing for us! We like to accomplish our own agenda, not somebody else's. We'd all rather be #1 instead of winding up at the bottom of the pile or at the end of the line. We naturally love being served by others. After all, serving others seems to be a lot of work and often makes us feel undignified and unappreciated. Where's the glory in humility? Where's the fun in that?

But Jesus teaches that even he, *"the Son of Man, did not come to be served but to serve."*[1]

Washing the feet of his disciples at the Last Supper was a wonderful object lesson for them, but how did Jesus serve us? He gave his life as a ransom for the world! He humbled himself even to death on the cross for us! And now Jesus watches over us and takes good care of us. As true God he possesses all the riches of the universe, *"yet for our sakes he became poor, so that we through his poverty might become rich."*[2]

St. Peter eventually learned this lesson. Many years later the Spirit would inspire him to write: *"Humble yourselves under God's*

---

[1] Matthew 20:28 and Mark 10:45

[2] 2 Corinthians 8:9, slightly altered from second person to third.

powerful hand so that he may lift you up at the appointed time." ³
So:

A Simple, Child-like Faith

begins with <u>humility</u>. After all, we poor, weak, sinful people are nevertheless <u>God's</u> people, and he is always ready and willing to lift us up with his almighty hand in the manner and at the time he knows is best for us.

A Simple, Child-like Faith

is humble before God; and it also:

Part 2: Values Children, Just as God Does.

Jesus said to the Twelve in:

Verses 5, 6, & 10: *⁵ "Whoever receives a little child like this one in my name receives me. ⁶ But, if anyone causes one of these little ones who believe in me to sin, it would be better for him to have a huge millstone hung around his neck and to be drowned in the depths of the sea. ...*

¹⁰ See to it that you do not look down on one of these little ones, because I tell you that their angels in heaven always see the face of my Father who is in heaven."

People would bring their little children to Jesus for him to lay his hand upon them and bless them. He even blessed their babies. All good parents strongly desire the blessing of Jesus Christ for their children!

One day Jesus' Twelve disciples decided that he was too busy to be bothered with children, so they shooed the kids and their parents away. Jesus was indignant and very displeased when he saw what was happening! He commanded: *"Let the little children come to me! Do not hinder them, because the kingdom of God belongs to such as these."* ⁴ Our Lord has always highly valued the little children.

After he rose from the dead, Jesus met with his disciples on the north shore of the Sea of Galilee. There he reinstated Peter, who, just

---

³ 1 Peter 5:6
⁴ Mark 10:14

a couple of weeks before, had vehemently denied three times that he even knew Jesus. But about two weeks later Jesus told him: *"Feed my lambs. ... Be a shepherd for my sheep. ... Feed my sheep."* [5] Lambs are little sheep. Lambs are included in the word sheep. Notice how Jesus singled out the lambs and placed them right up front when he told Peter *"Feed my lambs!"* Our Good Shepherd highly values little children.

When Jesus commissioned his Church to gather disciples from all the nations by baptizing them and by teaching them all his words, he did <u>not</u> say that they should baptize and teach only the adults. He included little children and even babies in the scope of his commission. Jesus said: *"Go and gather disciples from all nations."* [6] Our Lord has always highly valued little children. So does:

A Simple, Child-like Faith

which also:

Part 3: Fights Against the World's Temptations.

Jesus says in:

<u>Verse 7</u>: *Woe to the world because of temptations to sin. Temptations must come, but woe to that person through whom the temptation comes!*

Yes, as Jesus says, *"Temptations must come."* He concedes that in this broken, corrupt, sin-filled world there is no avoiding its temptations. Certainly we can avoid <u>many</u> temptations, but as long as we live in this fallen world we will certainly be faced with countless temptations to sin and to fall away from the one true God.

Now that does <u>not</u> mean that God sends temptations into our lives! Martin Luther correctly wrote that "God surely tempts no one to sin." [7] The author of every temptation and of every evil is always Lucifer — the Devil himself. He uses the things and the affairs and the distractions and the people and the pleasures and the problems of <u>this world</u> to drive wedges between us and our loving Creator and

---

[5] John 21:15-17

[6] Matthew 28:19

[7] Martin Luther, *Small Catechism*, in his definition of the Sixth Petition of our Lord's Prayer.

his holy Word. Satan even uses our own sinful flesh to weaken our connection to God and his holy Gospel, to make us love sinning, and to use the Gospel of forgiveness as if it were a sinning license.

Jesus teaches us to avoid Satan's temptations with:

A Simple, Child-like Faith.

How can we do that, since we're up against the Devil himself? If left to ourselves and to our own devices, we could never stand up against him. Satan is very powerful, and we would not stand a chance. But God has not left us to ourselves! We are not alone in this fight! God gave his angels charge over us so that Satan cannot harm us. The Archangel Michael leads the charge against our old evil Foe — and, as we sing in Luther's great hymn:

> The old evil Foe now means deadly woe;
> He can harm us none;
> He's judged — the deed is done!
> One little word can fell him! [8]

That little word is <u>Jesus</u>. Jesus has defeated our old evil Foe for us! So:

A Simple, Child-like Faith

Part 4: Trusts in Jesus for Salvation.

Jesus says in the last verse of our text:

<u>Verse 11</u>: *"The Son of Man came to save what was lost."*

You know what was lost? You were! I was! All of the little children were lost — just as every teenager and every adult in this world were all lost, too! Lost in the darkness of sin and doomed to suffer its eternal consequences — lost here in this world, and lost in the world to come. And there was nothing that any of us could do about it.

But praise our Lord Jesus for coming into this world to find us and save us! As the writer of the hymn *Amazing Grace* says:

---

[8] The closing words of stanza 3 of Martin Luther's hymn "A Mighty Fortress," #200 and #201.

I once was lost, but now I'm found....[9]

Though we were <u>lost</u> in our many sins, we have been <u>found</u> by the Good Shepherd who loves us wandering sheep so much that he willingly poured out his lifeblood on the cross for us. Jesus paid for the guilt of our sins and for the sins of the whole world. By his grace he sent the Holy Spirit into our hearts through this Gospel message — in his Holy Word, and in Holy Baptism. Through these simple means of grace, the Holy Spirit moved us to trust in Jesus for forgiveness and salvation.

A Simple, Child-like Faith

trusts in this Good News: *"God so loved the world that he gave his only-begotten Son, that whoever believes in him shall not perish but have eternal life."*[10] This is most certainly true!

So Jesus teaches us that:

A Simple, Child-like Faith

1) Is humble before almighty God,
2) Values children, just as God does,
3) Fights against the world's temptations, and
4) Trusts in Jesus for salvation.

May God bless us all with such:

A Simple, Child-like Faith.

AMEN.

---

[9] From stanza 1 of John Newton's (1725-1807) hymn "Amazing Grace," #379.
[10] John 3:16

Reformation Sunday

(October 31, or the last Sunday in October)

TEXT: Jeremiah 18:1-11

In the name of our Lord Jesus Christ, dear fellow heirs of the Lutheran Reformation:

A sculptor is an artist. A sculptor who makes round things out of clay is called a "potter." Pots are the typical product of the potter's wheel. You know how they work. The potter sits next to the horizontal wheel with a lump of clay in the center. As the wheel spins, the potter drizzles a little water on the clay and manipulates it with his hands, gradually sculpting something round. He continues until he has fashioned a nice pot — perhaps for some woman to use in her cooking, or perhaps for some man to use as a storage vessel, or for whatever purpose.

Every artist wants his workmanship to speak for itself. The ability and genius of an artist is known by the quality of his workmanship. If the workmanship is poor, or not quite what the potter had in mind, he smashes the clay even before it comes off of the wheel, and he starts over, reforming his lump of clay into something that pleases him.

It is <u>this</u> illustration that God uses in our text, and he uses it to teach his people a very important lesson! Listen to the Word of God as recorded by Jeremiah in chapter 18:

> *¹ This is the word that came to Jeremiah from the LORD: ² "Get up, and go down to the potter's house, and there I will reveal my words to you."*
>
> *³ So I went down to the potter's house, and he was making something on the wheel. ⁴ But the pot he was forming out of the clay was ruined as he shaped it with his hands, so the potter formed it into a different pot, whatever he saw fit to make.*
>
> *⁵ Then the word of the LORD came to me.*

⁶ "House of Israel, can I not do with you as this potter does?" declares the LORD. "See, like clay in the potter's hands, that is what you are in my hands, house of Israel. ⁷ One time I may say that a nation or a kingdom is to be uprooted, torn down, and destroyed, ⁸ but if that nation I spoke about repents of its evil, then I will relent and not bring the disaster I had planned to bring against it. ⁹ Another time I may say that a nation or a kingdom is to be built and planted, ¹⁰ but if they do what is evil in my sight by not listening to my voice, then I will not bring about the good I said I would do for them.

¹¹ "Now therefore say this to the men of Judah and to those who live in Jerusalem. This is what the LORD says. 'Look! I am forming a disaster against you. I am devising a plan against you. Turn from your evil ways, each of you, and reform your ways and your actions.'"

The Word of the Lord. Thanks be to God!

Like Clay in the Hands of a Potter,

Part 1: So Were the People in Jeremiah's Day!

With the Great Flood in Noah's day, God had cleansed this world from the vast majority of sinners. Afterwards, God commanded Noah's family to replenish the earth with people who would be faithful to God. Sad to say, within a few generations most of the human race was just as wicked as it had been before the Flood!

So God separated Abram, Isaac, and Jacob from most of the wicked peoples among whom they lived. He promised to send his Son through their bloodline to save the world from sin. He delivered their descendants from bondage in Egypt. He led them through the wilderness and gave them the land of Canaan, some of the best land in the Middle East. He blessed them and gave them a wonderful body of laws and promises which distinguished them from the wicked nations among whom they lived. He set up his chosen people as a light to enlighten the surrounding nations in the Way of salvation.

God sent them many prophets with his Word, and he sent many deliverers to rescue them from heathen persecutors and conquerors. God was forming them into his special holy people, preparing them for the arrival of his Messiah.

But they sinned. In fact, they repeatedly committed the same wicked and rebellious acts! Persistently they turned their backs on the God of Abram, Isaac, and Jacob. They intermarried with their heathen neighbors and adopted their gods and their wicked lifestyles. They became deeply involved in the pagan religions of the surrounding nations. Consistently they rejected God's covenant and turned to idol worship. So the LORD God used the Assyrian army to destroy the northern ten tribes of Israel in 722 B.C.[1] All that remained after their destruction was the one tribal territory of Judah, the land around Jerusalem.

Now here we are, a century and a quarter after the destruction of the ten northern tribes. The LORD has sent his prophet Jeremiah to the people of Judah with the very same message he had sent so many prophets to tell the ten northern tribes: "Repent! Turn away from worshiping false gods and turn back to me! If you do, I will forgive you and bless you. But if you do not repent, I'll destroy you, too! You will lose your nation, your land, and your freedom."

You see, just as a potter fashions a lovely new clay pot, God had been trying to fashion for himself a holy people; but over and over and over again his pot had become deformed. God's clay pot needed to be reformed! The only way to prevent his people of Judah from experiencing the destruction they deserved – just like their cousins to the north — was for the people of Judah to repent of their wickedness and return to the LORD for forgiveness and new life. That's the message of this text — especially the last verse:

Verse 11: *This is what the LORD says. "Look! I am forming a disaster against you. I am devising a plan against you. Turn from your evil ways, each of you, and reform your ways and your actions."*

Like Clay in the Hands of a Potter,

---

[1] In 722 B.C. Samaria, the capital city of the northern ten tribes of Israel, was destroyed by the Assyrian army led by their general Sennacherib.

Part 2: So Were the People in <u>Jesus'</u> Day.

Jesus went throughout the Holy Land, preaching and teaching: *"The kingdom of God is near! Repent, and believe the Gospel!"* [2] Jesus was trying to fashion for himself a Church which would be holy and sinless and radiant with God's glory. But the people in Jesus' day were far from holy. They did not love God most of all. They did not love their neighbor as much as they loved themselves.

So Jesus came into this world and went to the cross. There he poured out his life blood as God's sacrificial Lamb, atoning for the sins of the world. Then, on the third day, Jesus rose back to life! He gave to his Church the Sacrament of Holy Baptism to wash away the sins of his people and to fashion for himself a radiant people without spot or stain or any other blemish, but holy and blameless in God's sight.

When he ascended to his Father's right hand, Jesus sent the Comforter, the Counselor, the Holy Spirit to establish his New Testament Church and to fill our hearts and minds with his Word. It was the <u>Spirit</u> who reminded Jesus' apostles and evangelists of everything he had done and taught, and the Spirit inspired them to write down the words we call the New Testament.

On Pentecost, when the Spirit gave birth to the New Testament Church, it had one major flaw: The Church was composed of <u>sinners</u> from the very start — forgiven sinners, to be sure, but sinners nonetheless! And sinners err. That's what sinners do. They make mistakes. Over the centuries they are bound to believe and teach erroneously. Even before the death of the Apostles, some sinners had already begun to teach heresies. (For example, St. Paul had to struggle against the <u>Judaizers</u> and St. John had to struggle against the <u>Docetists</u>.)

Questions arose in the early Church about the nature of God and about the persons of Jesus and of the Holy Spirit. They struggled with questions such as these: How are the three persons of the Holy Trinity related? Is Jesus just a godly man and very God-like, or is Jesus truly God and truly human in one person? These were the biggest issues throughout the Christian Church for the first four and

---

[2] Cf. Matthew 4:17; Mark 1:15

a half centuries. Praise God that the Spirit moved the great Christian theologians to find the answers to these important questions in the divinely inspired Word of God! It was through those holy writings that God reformed his Church, providing the answers needed for faithful Christians to teach and believe correct doctrine.

Like Clay in the Hands of a Potter,
Part 3: So Were the People in Luther's Day.

God has always blessed his church beyond human imagination. For a thousand years, throughout the Middle Ages, nearly all of Europe was Christian — at least in name. Yet by the 1500s the Church of Luther's day had become very corrupt. The bishops had become princes and administrators rather than theologians and pastors. Countless superstitions arose during the Middle Ages, such as purgatory, the veneration of relics and dead saints — especially Jesus' mother Mary, the sale of forgiveness of sins for a donation to the church, the sale of indulgences and of masses to get out of purgatory earlier, and the teaching that every priest repeats Christ's sacrifice during every mass on every church's altar in order to atone for the sins of living people and the sins of all the dead whose souls are still in purgatory.

Many other false doctrines and ungodly practices had crept into the Church. Most insidious to the faith of God's people was the widespread teaching that people must save themselves from damnation by obedience to God's Law and especially to the Church's laws, rather than simply by trusting in Jesus for forgiveness of sins and eternal salvation.

The Church which the Holy Spirit had formed so purely on Pentecost had become thoroughly deformed by Luther's day. What the Christian Church needed was a re-formation! In his infinite wisdom and grace, God raised up Martin Luther and other reformers to reform his Church by pointing people back to the Bible as the only source for Christian faith and life. In the Bible they found a wonderful message from God himself — to learn that Jesus is the only hope of salvation for sinners, and that he has already done everything to win our salvation for us! Believe it, and receive it!

The people of the sixteenth century were:

Like Clay in the Hands of a Potter,

needing to be <u>re</u>formed by God himself. And:

Part 4: So Are <u>All</u> People in <u>Our</u> Day!

When each one of us was baptized, God claimed us as his own and declared us poor, miserable sinners to be his holy children. Yet since the day of our baptism we have proven ourselves to be <u>far</u> from holy! King David says it this way: *"Every one of them has turned away. Altogether they have become rotten. There is no one who does good. There is not even one."* [3]

So every one of <u>us</u> rotten sinners needs to be <u>re</u>formed! While it is true that *"The wages of sin is death,"* it is also true that *"the undeserved gift of God is eternal life in Christ Jesus, our Lord."* [4] *"For God did not send his Son into the world to condemn the world, but to save the world through him."* [5] And *"There is now no condemnation for those who are in Christ Jesus."* [6]

That's Great News! Our Creator is loving and merciful! Rather than damning us, he prefers to forgive our sins and to make us his special people for time and for eternity. He cleanses us of our guilt through faith in his Son Jesus. <u>De</u>formed by our own sinfulness, God <u>re</u>forms us through his holy Gospel into his own holy children, "that we should be his own, and serve him in everlasting righteousness, innocense, and blessedness." [7]

May God Almighty take each of us:

Like Clay in the Hands of a Potter

and make us beautiful in his eyes as he continues to reform us by his holy Gospel every day! In the name of our blesséd Redeemer Jesus. AMEN.

---

[3] Psalm 14:13. The last half of the verse is also written in Psalm 53:3 and Romans 3:12.

[4] Romans 6:23

[5] John 3:17

[6] Romans 8:1

[7] From Martin Luther's *Small Catechism*, definition of the Third Article of the Apostles' Creed.

All Saints Sunday

(November 1, or the first Sunday in November)

TEXT: <u>Selected Verses from Isaiah 26</u>

¹ On that day this song will be sung in the land of Judah.

> We have a strong city.
> God sets up salvation as its walls and ramparts.
> ² Open the gates,
> so that the righteous nation may enter,
> the nation that guards the truth.
> ³ You preserve perfect peace for the person whose resolve is steadfast,
> because he trusts in you.
> ⁴ Trust in the LORD forever,
> for YAH the LORD is the eternal Rock. . . .
>
> ⁸ Truly, LORD, we have waited for you on the path of your judgments.
> Your name and your renown are what our soul desires.
> ⁹ My soul longs for you during the night.
> My spirit within me looks for you early in the morning,
> because when your judgments are known on earth,
> the inhabitants of the world will learn what righteousness is. . . .
>
> ¹² O LORD, you establish peace for us.
> Everything we have done, you have accomplished for us.
> ¹³ O LORD our God, other lords besides you have ruled over us,
> but we honor only your name. . . .
>
> ¹⁹ But your dead ones will live.
> Their dead bodies will rise.
> Wake up and sing for joy,
> you who dwell in the dust,

> *because your dew will glisten like morning light,*
> *and the earth will give up the spirits of the dead.*
>
> ²⁰ *Go, my people, go into your rooms,*
> *and shut the doors behind you.*
> *Hide yourselves for a little while,*
> *until his wrath has passed over.*
> ²¹ *Look! The LORD is coming out of his place*
> > *to deal with the guilt of those who live on the earth.*
> *Then the earth will reveal the blood shed on it.*
> *It will no longer cover those who have been killed.* ✣

The Word of the LORD. Thanks be to God!

In the name of Jesus Christ, who has who has sanctified us and called us to be his saints by the working of his Holy Spirit, dear Christian friends:

Last Sunday we celebrated the anniversary of the Lutheran Reformation, and we were reminded that Martin Luther posted his *Ninety-Five Theses* on the eve of All Saints Day in 1517. All Saints Day was added to the Christian calendar in A.D. 835. During the fourteenth century, the prominence of the Roman Catholic invention of purgatory caused the next day, November 2nd, to be designated "All Soul's Day," or "Day of the Dead." (That's *"El Dia de los Muertos"* in the Spanish speaking world.)

That was two centuries before Luther. By that time the Catholic Church had developed the false teaching that only the holiest of Christians were "saints" — that they had performed so many good works during their lives in this world that they got to skip purgatory and go directly into heaven, but that the vast majority of Christian souls must stop off in purgatory for a few thousand or even millions of years to be punished for their many sins <u>before</u> getting into heaven. How long will those deceased Christians have to spend in purgatory? Only God knows that answer — not even the pope. However, according to Rome, the pope possesses Jesus' Keys, and that gives to the pope alone the power to grant people time off from purgatory for good behavior, that is, for doing certain things which Rome says are good works.

That promise of an early release or exemption from purgatory is called an indulgence. Of course, the Bible teaches nothing of the sort about these things. We Lutherans vigorously oppose the Catholic teachings about purgatory and indulgences because they violate the chief doctrine of the Christian faith, which is justification by God's grace alone through faith alone in Christ Jesus without any need for us to perform any good works to earn or deserve salvation. If a person goes to heaven, to God <u>alone</u> belongs <u>all</u> the glory! Nobody dare claim any credit at all for his own salvation, for that denies God's grace and robs him of his glory. Purgatory does <u>not</u> exist. It's just a money making invention of the Catholic Church.

So for Catholics November 1st became the day for celebrating the lives of their relatively <u>few</u> holy saints. That's what All Saints Day is all about. November 2nd became the day to celebrate the lives of all the rest — all of the other less-than-holy souls, and to pray for their deliverance from purgatory. That's what All Souls Day is all about.

The Lutheran Reformation was a <u>conservative</u> reformation! Luther and his fellow Lutheran reformers did <u>not</u> try to topple every teaching and practice of the Roman church. The Lutheran reformers only rejected those teachings and practices of the Catholic Church which were contrary to the Bible. The Lutherans kept all of the good Catholic practices which were useful for teaching the Gospel. The Lutherans entirely rejected All Souls Day and purgatory, and they restored All Saints Day to its original significance: an opportunity to teach what God's Word says about saints, especially those already in heaven, and to praise and thank God for the wonderful examples of Christian faith and life which they set for us.

We want to live as those saints in heaven did! We want to die as they did! We want to rise and go to heaven as they did! And someday, in God's own time, we want to be just as they are now — living forever with our Creator and Savior, with all of his angels, and with all of our fellow saints in heaven. Ah, yes, heaven — that perfect paradise where there is no more sin and none of the consequences of sin which we experience in this sin-cursed world.

So then, why bother observing the historic Festival of All Saints? In short, celebrating All Saints Day, or All Saints Sunday, is a very Lutheran thing to do! Hebrews 13:7 says: *"Remember your leaders, who spoke the word of God to you. Carefully consider the outcome of their way of life and imitate their faith."* Almost all of Jesus' apostles died as martyrs for their Christian faith and for proclaiming salvation through faith in the crucified and risen Lord Jesus. Again: *"Remember your leaders, who spoke the word of God to you. Carefully consider the outcome of their way of life and imitate their faith."*

Our text this morning is found in the prophet Isaiah, chapter 26, where God's prophet taught his people that:

The Ultimate Victory Belongs to God's Saints!

The prophet Isaiah was the most important pastor in Jerusalem seven hundred years before Christ. In this part of this very long book Isaiah has been talking about, not the Day of the Dead, but "the Day of the LORD" — that great Last Day when our LORD returns in judgment to rescue his people by defeating and destroying their enemies for the final time. That "Day of the LORD" will bring a very thorough judgment, but it will also bring a very perfect salvation from that judgment. Those who are condemned will spend eternity with the devil and his angels in hell, but those who are saved from that damnation will spend eternity in heaven with our Creator and Savior and with all of his saints.

In the chapter immediately preceding this text, Isaiah foretold God's judgment of Israel's primary enemy at that time — the Moabites, who lived just across the Jordan River and then a little south along the eastern shore of the Dead Sea. Isaiah prophesied that God would utterly defeat and destroy them and their wicked civilization, because for centuries they had persecuted and harassed God's chosen people.

Here in chapter 26 Isaiah promises that God will give the final victory to his faithful people. Then the prophet turns from speaking merely on a physical plain about the city of Jerusalem itself. He uses this occasion to speak metaphorically to all of God's faithful people everywhere about the new Jerusalem — the heavenly Jerusalem and those who live there with God.

Part 1: The Victory Belonged to God's Saints in the Past.

<u>Verse 13</u>: *O LORD, our God, other lords besides you have ruled over us, but your name alone do we honor.*

It's true. Other "lords" had indeed ruled over God's people in the Holy Land. The Egyptians, Philistines, Edomites, Moabites, and Assyrians come to mind immediately. And many others would rule over them in the future, such as the Babylonians, Ptolemies, Syrians, Macedonians, Seleucids, Romans, Idumeans, and even Muslims.

But the one true God always delivered his people from their enemies. He had made many promises to them and to their Patriarchs, to Abraham, Isaac, and Jacob — especially that greatest promise of all: to send his Messiah through their bloodline to save them from their sins, from death, and from the power of the devil, not with gold or silver, but with his holy, precious blood, and with his innocent suffering and death. All this God did so that all of his faithful people might live with him in his kingdom and serve him in everlasting righteousness, innocense, and blessedness.

In biblical times God repeatedly gave his saints victory over their enemies. And:

Part 2: The Victory belongs to God's Saints Right Now as Well.

We can be certain that our faithful God always takes care of his faithful people, delivering us from our greatest enemy, from the Devil himself, who is constantly going throughout this world like a roaring lion seeking human souls to devour. But:

Part 3: The Ultimate Victory Will Belong to All of God's Saints in the Future, Too!

Listen to how, in Verses 19 and 21, Isaiah teaches the physical resurrection of our bodies to everlasting life:

> *¹⁹ But your <u>dead will live; their bodies will rise</u>.*
> *<u>You who dwell in the dust, wake up and shout for joy</u>!*
> *Your dew is like the dew of Philistines morning; <u>the earth will give birth to her dead</u>. ...*

> ²¹ *See, the* LORD *is coming out of his dwelling to punish the people of the earth for their sins.*
> <u>*The earth will disclose the blood shed upon her; she will conceal her slain no longer.*</u>

So then you are God's saints right now! You are the people of God! You are people whose robes have been washed clean in the blood of the Lamb! You are the people who have been cleansed from the guilt of your sins by Baptism, *"the washing of rebirth and renewal by the Holy Spirit."*[1] Saints are <u>not</u> just the super-holy people who died long ago, who were so holy that their souls went straight to heaven without having to spend any time in purgatory. The Holy Spirit has made <u>you</u> God's saints! He has set <u>you</u> apart from the unbelieving world. He has worked in <u>your</u> heart true faith in Christ Jesus. He has caused <u>you</u> to believe in the Son of the living God and to find your confidence of eternal life in the Savior of the nations.

Trust in the LORD of salvation, the eternal God who took on human flesh and blood, and who did battle <u>for you</u> against your greatest enemy, the Devil himself. Jesus won the victory <u>for you</u> by never once caving in to any of Satan's temptations. And he won the victory <u>for you</u> by sacrificing his life on the cross to atone for every one of your sins, no matter how bad.

The most powerful proof of Jesus' victory and of our salvation is his own resurrection from the grave. Jesus' resurrection guarantees ours! His victory over death guarantees ours! As Isaiah says in verse 19: *"Your dead will live; their bodies will rise."* And as Jesus himself says: *"Because I live, you also will live."*[2]

Jesus made every one of us a <u>saint</u> by washing away our sins in Baptism. He continues to care for us and for all of his saints — for those of us who are still in this world, and for those who have gone on ahead into the new Jerusalem.

So rejoice that <u>you</u> are numbered among God's chosen saints! There's no purgatory for you! (It doesn't exist, anyway — regardless of what the pope says.) God will punish the wicked for their sins

---

[1] Titus 3:5
[2] John 14:19

forever in hell. But, as with all of God's saints, you will also rise to live forever with our Lord in heaven. Have a happy Festival of All Saints! AMEN.

Christ the King Sunday

(The Last Sunday of the Church Year)

TEXT: Daniel 7:13-14

¹³ I kept watching the night visions, and there, in the clouds of heaven, I saw one like a son of man coming. He came to the Ancient of Days, and he was brought before him. ¹⁴ To him was given dominion, honor, and a kingdom. All peoples, nations, and languages will worship him. His dominion is an eternal dominion that will not pass away, and his kingdom is one that will not be destroyed. ✡

The Word of the LORD. Thanks be to God!

In the name of Jesus, the King of kings and Lord of lords, dear Christian friends:

Today is the last Sunday of this church year. Our Scripture readings, sermons, and hymns over the past few Sundays have increasingly focused our thoughts on the end times — especially on Jesus' return on Judgment Day. It doesn't take much effort for us to look around and see all the evil in this world, to see the ravages of sin in the hearts and minds and lives of all people — even in our own. When we open our Bibles and read the many descriptions of the perfect paradise that awaits us in heaven, all of us Christians pray:

Come Back Soon, King Jesus!

Part 1: Come Back in the Same Way You Left Us!

Our Old Testament Lesson this morning serves as our sermon text. It's just two verses from the Book of Daniel, chapter 3. Daniel was not a prophet by profession. In fact, he was a very high ranking government official in the Neo-Babylonian empire — first under emperor Nebuchadnezzar, and now in the first year of the imperial reign of Belshazzar. The year was approximately 553 B.C.

One night, as Daniel lay on his bed, God gave him a series of visions, revealing to him the basic outline of the rest of world history.

Each major empire would eventually give way and be succeeded by another, until finally the Son of Man would triumph. When Daniel got up, he wrote down the main points of each of these visions. Listen again to his testimony in our Old Testament Lesson:

<u>Verse 13</u>: *I kept watching the night visions, and there, in the clouds of heaven, I saw one like a son of man coming. He came to the Ancient of Days, and he was brought before him.*

After Jesus suffered and died on the cross to pay for our sins and the sins of all mankind, he rose back to life. He appeared to many people on at least twenty two occasions! Our Savior had completed what he had come to do in this world, so he ascended to his heavenly throne in the presence of over a hundred of his disciples. They stared into the sky, gazing at the last spot where they had seen him disappear into the cloud. All of a sudden, two angels stood beside them and announced that someday *"This same Jesus, who has been taken up from you into heaven, will come back in the same way you have seen him go into heaven."*[1]

Jesus had promised his disciples that he would rise from the dead, and he did. He had promised that he would return to his Father's side in heaven, and he did. He promised that he would send the Holy Spirit to his Church to empower us to take Jesus' message to the whole world, and he did. He promised to go to prepare a place for us, and that's what he is doing right now. He promised that he would remain with us, never leaving us nor forsaking us, and he is fulfilling that promise even now. In short, Jesus has always kept every single one of his promises, and he will keep this final promise, too. Someday he will return on clouds of glory, just as he ascended into heaven; he will raise the bodies of all the dead and reunite them with their souls; he will judge all those who are still alive; he will consign the wicked to eternal flames; and he will take all of his faithful people into the eternal mansions of paradise. This is most certainly true!

Jesus always fulfills his promises. He promised to return when nobody is expecting it — and he will! So we Christians pray:

---

[1] Acts 1:11

Come Back Soon, King Jesus!

Come Back in the Same Way You Left Us! For we know what awaits us in the presence of our Creator and Savior, who is both Son of Man and the Son of God. We also pray:

Part 2: Come Back as Ruler of Your Kingdom!

Jesus <u>does</u> have a kingdom, you know, and he <u>does</u> reign over his kingdom. In fact, it is the eternal God himself, the Heavenly Father, the Ancient of Days, who bestowed this kingdom upon his only-begotten Son Jesus. That's what Daniel says in our text. He says in:

<u>Verse 14</u>: *To him was given dominion, honor, and a kingdom. All peoples, nations, and languages will worship him. His dominion is an eternal dominion that will not pass away, and his kingdom is one that will not be destroyed.*

In this vision God gave Daniel the privilege of seeing the coronation of Jesus Christ. This is what moved George Fridric Handel[2] to write in his masterpiece, *The Messiah*:

> King of kings and Lord of lords!
> King of kings and Lord of lords!
> And He shall reign forever and ever and ever.
> Hallelujah!

When Jesus stood before the Roman governor, Pontius Pilate asked him: *"Are you a king?"* Jesus responded:

> *"My kingdom is not of this world. If my kingdom were of this world, my servants would fight so that I would not be handed over to the Jews. But now my kingdom is not from here. ... I am, as you say, a king. For this reason I was born, and for this reason I came into the world, to testify to the truth. Everyone who belongs to the truth listens to my voice."*[3]

---

[2] Born in Germany in 1685 and named Georg Friedrich Händel; moved to England in 1712, anglicized his name to George Frideric Handel, and died in 1759.

[3] John 18:33-37

Think about that! Jesus has been given all authority, power, and glory. As he said after his resurrection: *"All authority on heaven and earth has been given to me. Therefore, go and gather disciples from all nations, baptizing them ... and teaching them...."*[4]

<u>How</u> does Jesus choose to rule? Not by force, nor by the sword, but by the still, small voice of his holy Word and the simple Gospel message in water, bread, and wine. Through these simple, loving Means of Grace, King Jesus establishes his everlasting kingdom. Rather than using physical force, King Jesus uses that one tool which is eternal, as he says: *"The heavens and the earth will pass away, but my words will never pass away."*[5]

All of us Christians are citizens of his kingdom, but do we honor Christ as our King? Do we always obey his holy Laws? Does his Word always rule in our hearts? Obviously, no. All too often we behave as though we had no king named Jesus. All too often we ignore our king and forget about our citizenship in his kingdom.

But praise be to Jesus that his holy Word continues and does not end with his Law. His Word also contains his Gospel! His Word includes the Good News that he has atoned for every one of our countless sins by his perfect life and by his sacrificial death on Calvary. Praise be to Jesus that, through faith in his substitutionary death and glorious resurrection, we have forgiveness of all our sins and the promise of eternal life to comfort us. Praise be to Jesus that our citizenship is in God's kingdom of grace here in this world, and in God's kingdom of glory in the world to come. And praise be to Jesus that he rose back to life from the dead as our victorious King! So we pray:

Come Back Soon, King Jesus!

Part 3: Come Back to Receive the Worship of All People!

Why did the Heavenly Father send his only-begotten Son into this sin-filled world? His purpose was to save the world from the eternal consequences of our sins, as St. John says: *"God did not send his Son into the world to condemn the world, but to save the world*

---

[4] Matthew 28:18-20

[5] Matthew 24:35

*through him."*⁶ So then, for whom did Jesus live, die, and rise again? For the world! For <u>all people</u>!

It's such a pity, such a waste, such a crying shame, that so many <u>billions</u> of people reject Jesus' free pardon and salvation by their impenitence and unbelief. They deny that Jesus is King of kings and Lord of lords. They deny Jesus the honor and worship that is due him. But when Jesus returns on Judgment Day, they will be caught off guard and have a rude awakening! St. Paul says it this way in:

<u>Philippians 2:8-11</u>: *⁸ [Jesus] humbled himself and became obedient to the point of death — even death on a cross. ⁹ Therefore God also highly exalted him and gave him the name that is above every name, ¹⁰ so that at the name of Jesus every knee will bow, in heaven and on earth and under the earth, ¹¹ and every tongue will confess that Jesus Christ is Lord, to the glory of God the Father.*

Yes, <u>every</u> knee will bow before him! <u>Every</u> tongue will confess that Jesus is Lord — and God will be glorified by them! Eventually, ultimately, finally, <u>all</u> people will come to know and acknowledge the truth about Jesus. For many billions it will be too late; their eternal destiny was already judged the moment they died. Yet for <u>us</u>, and for all who are still alive, there remains this time of grace — the opportunity to repent and believe the Gospel. We do not know — nobody but God does! — exactly when King Jesus will return on clouds of glory, but we do know that <u>he will</u> return.

So let us live our lives with one eye on our business and with one eye on the sky, for Christ will return as a thief in the night when he is least expected. Let us always be prepared to receive our Lord of glory who bought us with his lifeblood as the price.

The first time Jesus came into this world, he came in abject humility, but the next time he will come in glory. We who are citizens of his kingdom eagerly pray for his return:

Come Back Soon, King Jesus!

Come back in the same way you left us! Come back as Ruler of your kingdoms of power, grace, and glory! Come back soon, King Jesus,

---

⁶ John 3:17

and receive the worship of all people — the worship you so richly deserve, and all to the glory of our Heavenly Father! AMEN.

A Festival of Thanksgiving

TEXT: Matthew 6:24-34

²⁴ *"No one can serve two masters. Either he will hate the one and love the other, or he will be devoted to the one and despise the other. You cannot serve both God and mammon.*

²⁵ *"For this reason I tell you, do not worry about your life, what you will eat or drink, or about your body, what you will wear. Is not life more than food and the body more than clothing?* ²⁶ *Look at the birds of the air. They do not sow or reap or gather into barns, and yet your heavenly Father feeds them. Are you not worth much more than they?*

²⁷ *"Which of you can add a single moment to his lifespan by worrying?* ²⁸ *Why do you worry about clothing? Consider how the lilies of the field grow. They do not labor or spin,* ²⁹ *but I tell you that not even Solomon in all his glory was dressed like one of these.* ³⁰ *If that is how God clothes the grass of the field, which is alive today and tomorrow is thrown into the furnace, will he not clothe you even more, you of little faith?*

³¹ *"So do not worry, saying, 'What will we eat?' or 'What will we drink?' or 'What will we wear?'* ³² *For the unbelievers chase after all these things. Certainly your heavenly Father knows that you need all these things.* ³³ *But seek first the kingdom of God and his righteousness, and all these things will be given to you as well.* ³⁴ *So do not worry about tomorrow, for tomorrow will care for itself. Each day has enough trouble of its own."* ✠

The Gospel of our Lord. Praise be to you, O Christ!

In the name of Jesus, our crucified, risen, and ascended Savior, dear Christian friends:

Mrs. Sarah Hale is probably best known as the author of the poem "Mary Had a Little Lamb." Mrs. Hale was the editor of several women's magazines in the mid-nineteenth century, and she used her position to lobby many, many politicians to establish an annual national day of Thanksgiving on the fourth Thursday of November. She began this personal crusade of hers in 1846. After countless articles and editorials and letters and personal visits, she finally got her wish. In 1863, in the middle of the War Between the States, President Lincoln proclaimed a national day of Thanksgiving on the fourth Thursday of November. This annual celebration has continued uninterrupted ever since, except for 1939 when President Franklin D. Roosevelt moved it up a week to the <u>third</u> week in November. The American people ignored his decree and celebrated Thanksgiving in the usual manner on the <u>fourth</u> Thursday anyway; so the next year F.D.R. reversed his decision and the rest is history.

Though Thanksgiving is a <u>federal</u> holiday and not a <u>church</u> holyday, most churches throughout America take this as a cue to dedicate one day each year as a day to give prayers, praise, and thanksgiving to Almighty God for the countless blessings he has showered upon us again and again, year after year. Most of the crops have been harvested. As always, God continues to provide for us.

In spite of our many sins, God still blesses us — in more ways than we realize or recognize — especially here in the U.S.A. Do you realize that this is one of the very few nations where the poorest 1% of the population has a major obesity problem? It seems that everywhere else the rich are the fat cats and the poor are scrawny! God is truly blessing us much more than we realize or deserve.

Jesus preached these words of our text to perhaps a hundred or more of his disciples on the slopes of a small mountain on the northwest shore of the Sea of Galilee. It was a natural amphitheater. He preached uphill to them his "Sermon on the Mount," recorded by St. Matthew in chapters 5–7. Our sermon text is located right in the middle of that most famous of sermons. And in this text Jesus teaches us:

Don't Worry! Be Happy!

Now let's unpack our Gospel lesson just a little:

Verse 24: *No one can serve two masters. Either he will hate the one and love the other, or he will be devoted to the one and despise the other. You cannot serve both God and mammon.*

There is no <u>good</u> <u>one</u> <u>word</u> translation for *mammon*. It's an Aramaic term for worldly wealth and property. The phrase "God and *mammon*" means the Creator and the creation. Jesus says that you cannot serve both. One of them will occupy first place in your heart, so the other one cannot. So which is more important to you — God, or the stuff that God has created? Do you love God most of all, or do you love the things he has made most of all? Jesus teaches us the importance of making that distinction. Loving and serving God most of all is <u>keeping</u> the First Commandment. Loving and serving anyone or anything else most of all is <u>breaking</u> the First Commandment.

Verses 25-26: *²⁵ For this reason I tell you, do not worry about your life, what you will eat or drink, or about your body, what you will wear. Is not life more than food and the body more than clothing? ²⁶ Look at the birds of the air. They do not sow or reap or gather into barns, and yet your heavenly Father feeds them. Are you not worth much more than they?*

Don't Worry! In this section of his Sermon on the Mount, Jesus teaches this over and over again. **Don't Worry!** Instead, **Be Happy!** Aren't you worth a whole lot more to God than a bunch of birds and flowers and grass? Of course you are! Arguing from the lesser to the greater: Since God feeds them and clothes them and provides for them, don't you think that he'll do even more for <u>you</u>?

Just how valuable are you to God? Think of what the Lord has done for you and for me! He looked down from heaven and saw us poor, miserable sinners doomed for damnation, and he rescued us. He saved us! He sacrificed his only begotten Son Jesus on the cross to atone for our countless sins, and he raised him back to life on the third day to declare us forgiven. He promised to return some day to take us to the paradise which he is preparing for us right now. He sent the Holy Spirit into our souls through his Word and through Baptism. He washed away our sins and made us his own beloved children for time and for eternity. And as long as we remain in this world, he takes wonderful care of us and provides for our every need.

Jesus asks us in:

Verses 27-30: *²⁷ Which of you can add a single moment to his lifespan by worrying? ²⁸ Why do you worry about clothing? Consider how the lilies of the field grow. They do not labor or spin, ²⁹ but I tell you that not even Solomon in all his glory was dressed like one of these. ³⁰ If that is how God clothes the grass of the field, which is alive today and tomorrow is thrown into the furnace, will he not clothe you even more, you of little faith?*

Again, Jesus teaches us: **Don't Worry! Be Happy!** After all, what good will worrying do? Will it help you live longer? Of course not. Will it improve your wardrobe? Obviously not. And aren't you more important to God than the beautiful lilies and grass in the fields? Of course you are. The lilies and the grass are here today and gone tomorrow, but not so with us! God knows what we need to survive and thrive. Jesus says:

Verses 31-32: *³¹ So do not worry, saying, "What will we eat?" or "What will we drink?" or "What will we wear?" ³² For the unbelievers chase after all these things. Certainly your heavenly Father knows that you need all these things.*

You see, these are things that the heathen chase. It's what their lives are all about. But we are different! We are the children of God! Our Heavenly Father already knows that we need food, clothing, and shelter. He already promises to give us our daily bread. So **Don't Worry** about these things! Instead, Jesus tells us in the next verse what our primary pursuit must be:

Verse 33: *Seek first the kingdom of God and his righteousness, and all these things will be given to you as well.*

"Seek first the kingdom of God and his righteousness," Jesus says. Make sure that you are in *the kingdom of God* — that you are and remain a citizen of his kingdom, that his holy Word rules in your heart, in your mind, and in your life. Then keep on seeking *his righteousness* by making certain that you don't fall away from God's kingdom into gross sin, impenitence, and unbelief, thereby forfeiting

your citizenship. Trust in God to provide everything that you need as well, because that is exactly what Jesus promises. He says: *"All these things will be given to you as well."* So just make sure to <u>be</u> and <u>remain</u> a faithful citizen of God's kingdom. If you do, you can be confident that God will also give you everything that he knows you need — and you can **Be Happy!**

Jesus concludes this section of his most famous sermon with:

<u>Verse 34</u>: *So do not worry about tomorrow, for tomorrow will care for itself. Each day has enough trouble of its own.*

He concludes by returning full circle to his theme: **Don't Worry!** Instead, **Be Happy!**

Trust in the Lord Jesus who lived, died, and rose for you. Trust in the God who never turns his back on his people, the God who has always come through for his faithful people, the God who is always faithful to his promises. **Don't Worry!** Instead, focus on God's many, many blessings, and you will **Be Happy** this Thanksgiving and every day! AMEN.

Soli Deo Gloria!

("Glory to God Alone!")

ABOUT THE AUTHOR

David George Peters is a Christian pastor and historical theologian. A graduate of Martin Luther Academy (New Ulm, Minnesota) and Northwestern College (Watertown, Wisconsin) with a Bachelor of Arts in classics, history, and religious studies, he earned the Master of Divinity and Master of Sacred Theology degrees at Wisconsin Lutheran Seminary (Mequon, Wisconsin). He studied Latin American culture and language at the Academia Latinoamericana de Español (Quito, Ecuador). His doctoral studies at Marquette University (Milwaukee, Wisconsin), focused on historical theology — especially the Dead Sea Scrolls, the early Church fathers, and the 16th century Reformations. He is a fellow of the Center for Reformation Research (St. Louis, Missouri), a former consulting editor for the annual *Luther Digest*, and a former editor of the *LSI Journal*, published quarterly by the Lutheran Science Institute.

With a strong background in the languages of biblical scholarship — Greek, Hebrew, Latin, and German — as well as Spanish — his theological studies are wide ranging and multi disciplinary. He is particularly interested in how we speak about the triune nature of God and about the dual natures in Christ, in Bible translation, in New Testament exegesis and textual criticism, and in the theology of the early Church fathers and the 16th century reformers.

For over three decades Rev. Peters has served congregations of the Wisconsin Evangelical Lutheran Synod in Nebraska, Kansas, Ohio, Wisconsin, and Minnesota. He also served for over two decades as an adjunct instructor in Lutheran elementary and high schools.

Rev. Peters is married and has been blessed with three children and seven grandchildren.

www.ingramcontent.com/pod-product-compliance
Lightning Source LLC
LaVergne TN
LVHW051116080426
835510LV00018B/2064